Marcelo Zigaran

Powers of Music

Marcelo Zigaran

Powers of Music

A Psychoanalytic Investigation about Music and Meaning

VDM Verlag Dr. Müller

Imprint

Bibliographic information by the German National Library: The German National Library lists this publication at the German National Bibliography; detailed bibliographic information is available on the Internet at http://dnb.d-nb.de.

Any brand names and product names mentioned in this book are subject to trademark, brand or patent protection and are trademarks or registered trademarks of their respective holders. The use of brand names, product names, common names, trade names, product descriptions etc. even without a particular marking in this works is in no way to be construed to mean that such names may be regarded as unrestricted in respect of trademark and brand protection legislation and could thus be used by anyone.

Cover image: www.purestockx.com

Publisher:
VDM Verlag Dr. Müller Aktiengesellschaft & Co. KG, Dudweiler Landstr. 125 a, 66123 Saarbrücken, Germany,
Phone +49 681 9100-698, Fax +49 681 9100-988,
Email: info@vdm-verlag.de

Copyright © 2008 VDM Verlag Dr. Müller Aktiengesellschaft & Co. KG and licensors
All rights reserved. Saarbrücken 2008

Produced in USA and UK by:
Lightning Source Inc., La Vergne, Tennessee, USA
Lightning Source UK Ltd., Milton Keynes, UK
BookSurge LLC, 5341 Dorchester Road, Suite 16, North Charleston, SC 29418, USA

ISBN: 978-3-639-01263-7

ACKNOWLEDGEMENTS

I would like to express my deepest gratitude to Professor Vagram Saradjian, my cello "Maestro" for all his teaching and guidance. A special thanks to my philosophy professor and friend, Dr. Cynthia Freeland, for her support in my topic, our discussions and her help during the whole process of my dissertation. I also would like to deeply thank my friend psychoanalyst, Guillermo Vilela, for sharing his psychoanalytic expertise, for all our brainstorm meetings, and his full support in my project. Finally, I would like to thank my wife, Patricia, for always accompanying me in the pursuit of my dreams.

TABLE OF CONTENTS

INTRODUCTION	1
CHAPTER I: JULIA KRISTEVA'S PSYCHOANALYTIC THEORY OF MUSIC	5
Jacques Lacan	8
Ferdinand de Saussure and Language	10
Lacan and Language	11
Kristeva's Theories of Music	15
Preliminary Conclusions	24
CHAPTER II: DIDIER-WEILL AND MUSIC AS AN EXPRESSION OF A DRIVE	26
A Contribution to the Question of the Invocative Drive	33
The Blue Note	37
Music and Time	39
Preliminary Conclusions	41
CHAPTER III: FROM THE SUBJECT TO THE MUSIC	45
The Sublime: Kant and Later Thinkers	60
A New Conception of Aesthetics	66
Preliminary Conclusions	70
CONCLUSION	71
The Performing Experience	74
BIBLIOGRAPHY	77

To my beloved Patricia and my little Sebastian

Introduction

This study is an interdisciplinary investigation of music and meaning using the framework of psychoanalysis. Within this framework, the study will also reflect the perspective of the performer. It will address questions such as: What is the power of music? Why, for many of us, is music of such importance as to give meaning to our lives? What makes a performer to dedicate his life to sound and to music? Ultimately, what does it mean to give a meaningful performance?

I have always thought that conventional musical analysis, whether it is harmonic, formal, or counterpoint analysis, never satisfactorily addresses the deep question of why music affects us so profoundly. Why does performing and listening to music engage us so emotionally that all of a sudden we might think: "What is happening to me?","Why are my emotions so powerful that I have the sensation of going to another world?" My comments will focus on discussing music from the standpoint of psychoanalysis because I find this approach insightful. It may prove helpful to understanding our relationship with music, whether we are listeners, performers or composers.

This thesis will be a contribution to understanding the performance experience through the lens of psychoanalysis, with an emphasis on the performer's point of view. Although some previous works have used psychoanalytic theories to discuss music, there are, to my knowledge, no more than a few works relating musical performance to the concepts of two important psychoanalysts: Julia Kristeva and Alain Didier-Weill.

Kristeva and Didier-Weill, psychoanalysts in the tradition of the French thinker Jacques Lacan, have both dedicated numerous books and essays to music and art. After an introduction to Freudian and Lacanian principles and their impact in our culture, I will proceed to examine the works of Kristeva and Didier-Weill for some clues to aspects of the performing experience, music and meaning, and meaningful performance. I plan to create a dialectical structure between the psychoanalytic texts explored and the thoughts and experiences narrated by different philosophers and musicians, including my teachers and myself.

The general structure of the dissertation is laid out in three main chapters. The first chapter will deal with Kristeva's work and its relationship with music. This chapter will focus on aspects of musical and artistic creativity that are closely related to the pre-oedipical, pre-linguistic phase. To perform a musical work is for many of us an attempt to express in our own way what the composer wrote; but this leads to the question, is music a language? Kristeva develops a conception of music as a drive and this may open the door for us to think about music, the sublime and the meaning of music.

The second chapter will elaborate on Didier-Weill's contribution to the understanding of music and the individual. With Weill, we will see music in relation to the individual (or a "subject" as it is referred to in psychoanalytic jargon), considering music, sound and their relevance in our human constitution. Why is it that so many times when we perform, we feel as if we were transported by music to other places? When performing, are my musical expressions, emotions and gestures an expression of myself in response to the music? Or during that experience, are my body and music the same thing? Didier-Weill describes music as the expression of a drive. My study of Didier-Weill will focus on his concepts of the "Blue note" and "the invocative drive", terms that I will explain in detail.

The third chapter will discuss musical aesthetics, summarizing how insights from psychoanalysis in the previous two chapters can be related to the aesthetics of music. In other words, psychoanalytic contributions to the understanding of music and performance through theories of subjectivity may be relevant but they also have their limits. For example, Kristeva's and Didier-Weill's works present a fascinating study of music in relation to the individual. However, they do not focus on music as an object of study, rather on the subject of the unconscious.

This chapter then will suggests some conclusions and raise some tensions to be further explored. One of these is the need to consider a new aesthetics, a new regimen of the sensible. Through the study of philosophers, theorists and musicians I will present an account of aesthetics as no longer simply a "theory of nice feelings" (as Hegel put it) but a complex philosophy of art: it involves interpretation, criticism and reflection upon works of art. A work of art, such as a symphony, has an existence, a history and a place that constitute it as the object of the aesthetic experience. Having said that, this document will stress the point that psychoanalysis presents us with a new way of looking at things--not only at music or art. It is in this way the departure point for an aesthetic revolution, in the sense of a new regimen of what we hear (and see) in the world. We can then decide in a different way what belongs to art and what does not, arriving at a new "regimen of the sensible", as Jacques Ranciere puts it in his book *The Division of the Sensible*.

CHAPTER I:

Julia Kristeva's Psychoanalytic Theory of Music

Although Freud wrote virtually nothing about music, many psychoanalysts who followed him did. Julia Kristeva is one of them. I this chapter I will present an introduction to some of her theories, particularly those related to the aesthetics of music. She, like other post-Freudians, considered music as a direct access route to the dimension of the unconscious. Coriat explains,

> Music reproduces emotional situations in a more direct way than can be done by any other form of art or any intellectual processes. It creates not only highly emotional reality but also the highest degree of unreality because it is marked by the absence of objective contents to which emotions can be linked. [1]

Music, in effect, has the ability to circumvent the external world of objects. Whether performing or listening to it, music takes us to a world devoid of reference to real objects.

Most poststructuralist writers consider music to originate within the primacy of the mother's voice for the newborn infant. They conceive the mother's voice as a sonorous envelope surrounding the newborn infant. By studying the relation of music to

---

[1] I. H. Coriat, "Some aspects of a Psychoanalytic Interpretation of Music", *Psychoanalytic Review*, Vol. XXXII, no. 1, 1945, p. 409.

subjects, it is possible to gain a new understanding of music that could be helpful for us as performers, composers, and listeners. Kristeva's views are a major contribution in this direction.

Julia Kristeva was born in Bulgaria in 1941. She was educated by nuns, but within the educational system of the communist party children's and youth groups. Her first job was as a journalist in a communist youth newspaper while pursuing literary studies at university. In 1966, Kristeva went to Paris for her doctoral studies in French literature. Her thesis director was Roland Barthes. She also held the position of research assistant at Claude Levis-Strauss's lab of social anthropology. Kristeva quickly became an important figure in the Parisian intellectual scene of the late 1960s and since that time her writings in linguistics, philosophy, psychoanalysis and semiology have influenced many areas of Western culture.

In 1973, at a lecture on psychoanalysis and politics in Milan, Kristeva said: "I never intended to follow a correct Marxist line, and I hope I am not correctly following any other line whatsoever."[2] The following year, her doctoral dissertation, *The Revolution of Poetic Language*, was published. As a result of this, she was offered a teaching position in linguistics at the University of Paris, where she still teaches. By 1979 she had also completed her training in psychoanalysis and in 1997 she was awarded the prestigious *Legion d'Honneur*. Since then she has been a frequent lecturer in New York (at Columbia University) and at psychoanalytic/literary conventions in Paris, London, Barcelona, and other European cities.

---

[2] Armando Verdiglione, *Psychanalyse et politique* (Paris: editions Seuil, 1974), p. 73

Kristeva is now an intellectual figure of international renown, a psychoanalyst, writer and literary critic. She adopts the classical terms of psychoanalytic theory. For her, psychoanalysis is the only discipline capable of restoring meaning to the lives of individuals in Western culture. Her work spans more than thirty years. During this time, Kristeva became recognized for her innovative concepts and conceptual coherence. Her work impresses many readers as a vast integrated work-in-progress of cultural critique. As Barthes described her, "Julia Kristeva always destroys the latest preconception, the one we thought we could be comforted by, the one of which we could be proud."[3]

Kristeva's work has included distinctive shifts over the years, from linguistics, structuralism, post-structuralism to an increasing focus in psychoanalysis as the ultimate frame of reference to discuss cultural issues. It is impossible to understand her theories if one leaves out Freudianism. Furthermore, a very precise post-Freudian school constitutes her theoretical background: namely, Lacan's readings of Freud.

Freud introduced the idea of the human self, or subject, as radically split, divided between the two realms of conscious and unconscious. On the one hand, our usual (Western humanist) ideas of self or personhood are defined by operations of consciousness, including rationality, free will, and self-reflection. For Freud, Lacan,

Kristeva and for psychoanalysis in general, however, actions, thought, belief, and the concepts of "self" are all determined or shaped by the unconscious and its drives and desires.

---

[3] Roland Barthes, "L'Etrangere," *Quinzaine Litteraire*, May 1-15, 1970, pp. 19-20.

Jacques Lacan

Jacques Lacan (1901-1981) revolutionized psychoanalysis and also considerably influenced other areas of culture with his "return to Freud."[4] He is considered the one of the leading figures in articulating Freud essential message, so as to rediscover Freud's legacy during a time when psychoanalysis had come under criticism from the scientific community. Freudian psychoanalysis had undergone critics and complaints of a society that rejected and became intolerant of the truths revealed by its practice and research. One of the most important psychoanalytic findings is that the boundaries between normal and abnormal are very thin. For example, the union of men and women is not necessarily "natural". Psychoanalysis created a cultural impact, erasing the comforting ideas of keeping limits between normal and abnormal, between virtuous and pervert, between good and bad. Psychoanalytic practice reveals that we are all "built" by the same principles and processes. After all, we are not as different as we would like to think we are. This is one important point in this study regarding the relationship of individuals with music as something structural and the idea of a musical meaning as I will point out later on this work.

When Lacan first encountered Freud's theories in the late 1930s, he was already an established psychiatrist and psychoanalyst in France. It was his combination of the theoretical and the clinical that would become Lacan's practice and inform what he would call his "return

---

[4] Jacques Lacan, *Ecrits,* (Paris: Seuil, 1966), p. 509.

to Freud." In his lifetime, Lacan extended the field of psychoanalysis into philosophy, linguistics, literature and mathematics, through close readings of Freud and continued clinical practice. Lacan attracted philosophers, linguists, and other thinkers to his renowned weekly seminar at St. Anne's Church, in Paris. Barthes, Foucault, Levi-Strauss, and Althusser sat in his audience and were influenced by his work. From this lecture series came what is perhaps his most celebrated work, *Écrits* (1966).

Lacan's seminars in the 1950's were one of the formative environments of the currency of philosophical ideas that dominated French letters in the 1960's and 70's, and which has come to be known in the Anglophone world as 'post-structuralism'. Both

inside and outside of France, Lacan's work has also been profoundly important in the fields of aesthetics, literary criticism and film theory.

With Lacan, as well as with Kristeva, language is considered to be the foundation of the human. The individual, in their view, is the subject that speaks. They both are post-structuralists in the sense that they focus on a de-centered subject, a subject divided by the appearance of the unconscious.

The unconscious is an abstract human dimension that reveals itself in our dreams, slips of the tongue, free association, jokes and negation; it is the place of our "desire"[5]. This is the

---

[5] Lacan states that desire is the desire of the Other. To put it roughly, Lacan's theory does not deny that infants are always born into the world with basic biological needs that need constant or periodic satisfaction but however stress that from a very early age, the child's attempts to satisfy these needs become caught up in the dialectics of its exchanges with others.

state of "nature," which has to be broken up in order for culture to be formed. This is true in both Freud's psychoanalysis and in Lacan's: in order to enter into civilization, the infant must separate from his mother and form a separate identity. That separation entails some kind of loss. That loss creates desire, a desire that cannot ever be fulfilled. The object of psychoanalysis is to study these psychical representations of absence, of things and experiences which, for one reason or another, remain lost or unrealized. Psychoanalysis is a practice that tries to bring into consciousness the repressed desires of the patient. Its practice differs from the practices of natural science

As opposed to traditional science, for psychoanalysis hearing is more important than seeing. Lacan's thesis is that Freud's insight into the nature of the talking cure was an insight into the way the laws of language work. The basis of these laws was established by Ferdinand de Saussure.[6]

Ferdinand de Saussure and language

According to Saussure, there is a distinction between a word in language and the object invoked by the word. The understanding of a word is related to the context of that language. The meaning of the words is not determined or fixed by external reality. Saussure accomplishes this transformation specifically in the redefinition of the linguistic "word," which he describes as

---

[6] The Swiss linguist Ferdinand de Saussure (1857-1913) is widely considered to be the founder of modern linguistics.

the linguistic "sign" and defines in functionalist terms. The sign, he argues, is the union of a concept, the *signified* [*signifié*], *and* a sound image, the *signifier* [*signifiant*]. By the term signifier, Saussure means not only the sound of the word itself, but also the psychological image of the sounds constituted in the experience of an individual. As Shepherdson and Wicke say, "In other words, the 'meaning' of words are in no way intrinsic to the sound of words...we only recognize sounds as meaningful in terms of their relationship of difference from other sounds...meaningful by the structure of language."[7]

Lacan and Language

Following Saussure, Lacan went further and determined that language produces a complete break with material reality. While for Freud there was some interaction between the material realities of bodies, Lacan emphasized that material realities can only be *experienced* through language.[8] He felt that Freud had understood that human psychology is linguistically based, but would have needed Saussure's vocabulary and structuralist concept of language as a system of differences to articulate the relationship between language and material reality. In

---

[7] John Shepherd and Peter Wicke, *Music and Cultural Theory,* (Malden, Massachusetts: Blackwell Publishers, 1997), p. 25.

[8] For Lacan the link between signifier and signified is so precarious that whereas Saussure saw the whole system as more or less grounded (though the possibility of slippage constituted his great contribution to twentieth-century linguistics), Lacan sees only occasional points of stability.

Les Psychoses: Seminar III, Lacan claims that the unconscious is "structured like a language," and governed by the order of the signifier.

Lacan holds that language belongs to the Symbolic order, one of three orders that constitute the subject in Lacanian psychoanalysis, (the other two are the Imaginary and the Real). For Lacan, submission to the rule of language itself--which he calls the law of the father-- is required in order to enter into the Symbolic order. He means by this that to become a speaking subject, you have to be subjected to, you have to obey, the laws and rules of language. Lacan designates the idea of the structure of language, and its rules, as specifically paternal.

To define the Imaginary, Lacan tells us that the idea of a self is created through an imaginary identification with the image in the mirror. The realm of the Imaginary is where the alienated relation of self to its own image is created and maintained. The Imaginary is a realm of images, whether conscious or unconscious. It is pre-linguistic and pre-oedipal. The mirror image, the whole person the baby mistakes as itself, is known in psychoanalytic terminology as an "ideal ego," a perfect whole self who has no insufficiency. This "ideal ego" becomes internalized; we build our sense of "self," our "I"dentity, by (mis)identifying with this ideal ego. By doing this, we imagine a self that has no lack, no notion of absence or incompleteness. The fiction of the stable, whole, unified self that we see in the mirror becomes a compensation for having lost the original oneness with the mother's body. According to Lacan, we lose our unity with the mother's body, the state of "nature," in order to enter culture, but we protect ourselves from the knowledge of that loss by misperceiving ourselves as not lacking anything-- as being complete.

The Real for Lacan is the unnamable reality, the one that cannot be expressed in words, it is always present but continually mediated through the Imaginary and the Symbolic. Lacan's theory starts with the idea of the Real; this is the union with the mother's body, which is a state of nature, but it must be broken up in order to build culture. Once you move out of the Real, you can never get back to it, but you always want to. This is the source of the first idea of an irretrievable loss or lack at the center of every subject in Lacan's view.

Since we cannot access the Real, we only have access to a chain of signifiers and no signified. For Lacan, there are no signified; there is nothing that a signifier ultimately refers to. What we consider reality is the result of the interaction of the symbolic world and the fragmentations of the Imaginary

One of Lacan's crucial findings is that because of this autonomy of the signifier we also lose our own body. Our body becomes the expression of a symptom. This means that the repression the individual suffers (in fact, the signified which has undergone repression) remains present in the body. For psychoanalytic psychopathology, the body itself 'speaks'. The corporal symptom is over-determined by a complex symbolic network and by language. Discerning the syntactic laws of this bodily language is the way to resolve the symptom. Thus for psychoanalysis, phenomena such as depression, eating-disorders, anxiety, and many others illnesses are the result of signifiers introduced in our body by mechanisms of repression. So we lose our body, we cannot feel it. We feel instead a cultural body mediated by the significant-signifier dimension.

Lacan's world presents us with concept of the individual whose subjectivity is not something given. To the contrary, subjectivity is continually striven for. Psychoanalysis tries to help people to find their unconscious desire, the one that by their history defines their subjectivity.

We can conclude this brief exploration of Lacan's theories by saying that his work presents a model to understand how the process of signification is connected to process of subjectivity. Furthermore, his theories open the door to conceive music as "circumventing the world of objects and language."[9] Music then can be studied as a practice with its own distinctive relation to the unconscious, psycho-sexual processes and the world of emotions.

The work of Saussure offers specific possibilities for a structuralist analysis of music. In the same way that words acquire meaning in relation to the structure of language, sounds acquire meaning in relation to the structure of music. Saussure and other structuralists consider human beings to be the producers and the product of a culture. His theory however, does *not* support treating music as a language. Shepherd and Wicke comment,

> Most musicians and musicologists experience difficulty with the idea that music's meanings are somehow arbitrary in their relationship to music's sounds... [because] This idea seems to lead to the inevitable conclusion that music is somehow the product of processes and forces extrinsic to

---

[9] See Shepherd and Wicke, p. 57.

> it...the presumed immanence of music's meanings to music's sounds becomes an effective mechanism in defending the integrity of music as a distinct form of human expression and signification.[10]

Kristeva's Theories of Music

With this linguistic-philosophic-psychoanalytic background we can now proceed to consider Kristeva's theories of music and their impact on contemporary theorists and philosophers. The first step is to determine to what extent music is a language. Kristeva mentions that the similarities of the two systems are considerable. "Verbal language and music are both realized by utilizing the same material (sound) and by acting on the same receptive organs."[11] The two signifying systems are organized according to the 'principle of difference' of their components. [12] However, this principle applies differently in each system. Music does not have the binary phonematic differences (linguistic phonematic units) that language does. Instead, as Kristeva explains, "the musical code is organized by the arbitrary and cultural (imposed within the framework of certain civilization) difference between various vocal values: notes." According to her, this difference is of capital importance because it leads to the

---

[10] Shepherd and Wicke, p. 27.

[11] Julia Kristeva, *Language the Unknown: An initiation into Linguistics,* tr. Anne M. Menke (New York: Columbia University Press, 1989), p.309.

[12] See Shepherd and Wicke, p. 101.

conclusion that "while the fundamental notion of language is the communicative function, and while it transmits a meaning, music is a departure from this principle of communication."[13]

In other words, Kristeva is saying that music transmits a message between a subject and an addressee, but we cannot say that music communicates a precise meaning. She considers that the emotional content or message that a musical work offers is the result of a "subjective interpretation given within the framework of a cultural system rather than the result of a 'meaning' implicit in the message"[14]. She cites Stravinsky who wrote, "I consider music, in its essence, as powerless to express anything at all: a feeling, an attitude, a psychological state, a phenomenon of nature, etc. Expression has never been the immanent property of music."[15]

I do not agree with Stravinsky but it is interesting to note that Kristeva herself will vary her position. So far Kristeva agrees with Barthes that "music takes us to the limit of the system of the sign,"[16] in the sense that music is a system of differences that is not a system that means [something]. In other words, although music seems to transmit a message, as Barthes says "it speaks but says nothing"[17], because it is no longer linguistic, but corporeal.

Kristeva's view (like Barthes' and Lacan's, for that matter) although profound, reproduces the hegemony of language in the sense of denying music of any ultimate meaning.

---

[13] Kristeva, cited above, p.309.

[14] Ibid.

[15] Igor Stravinsky, quoted in Kristeva, p.309.

[16] Kristeva, p.309

[17] Barthes, quoted in Kristeva, p. 309.

Kristeva seems to consider music as an inferior system to language. While acknowledging her observations as relevant to our understanding of music, some musical theorists have begun to confront the hegemony of language as a frame of reference. Shepherd and Wicke claim that while it is true that sounds in music do not signify in the same way as they do in language, "it is possible to conceive of a different order of differences for music." [18]

The above quotations belong to her semiological approach and the study of linguistics, in which the symbolic world is sovereign over cultural life. However Kristeva expresses a very different conception of the nature of music and other arts. Since *The revolution of poetic language* her writing has became more psychoanalytic. I will now turn to those studies as well as to some excerpts from *Le temps sensible (1994), a* more recent work.

Kristeva's psychoanalytic position is a continuation of the theoretical groundwork laid down by Freud and Lacan. It is based on a Freudian theory of the subject and its origins. In these theories language is considered a structure rather than an object. This is also the position assumed in this study: music as structure, understood as having different simultaneous processes rather than as a static object of study. In traditional philosophy, the "object," the passive thing that serves as the content of conscious observation, is contrasted with the "subject," the conscious agent who observes the object. In attempting to understand the relationship between subject and object, psychoanalysis describes objects that have been cathected, invested with libidinal energy. These objects can be music other people (the "object

---

[18] Shepherd and Wicke, p.100.

of one's affections"), or anything else (including abstract concepts like freedom or justice) that serves as a focal point of desire. This position brings us back to the subject.

Music involves a subject that performs, composes or listens. And this subject is a divided, de-centered subject, in the sense that it is split into the level of the conscious and unconscious. Anne-Marie Smith in her study of Kristeva tells us,

> The theory that language owes its vitality and capacity for renewal to this infiltration of subversive forces [unconscious drives] which rock the status quo also means that a culture is kept alive and owes its dynamism to artistic activity and an individual's health is bound up with her capacity to create and imagine.[19]

This is Kristeva's contribution in thinking about literature, music and other arts: they are forms of creation for our unnamable thoughts. Music can be conceived as a result of unconscious, subjective and social relations. Instead of being a unified, aestheticized object, music becomes a *practice*. Music is living thing through which the subject can sustain interaction. As Kristeva tell us, "it becomes a means of transforming natural and social resistances, limitations and stagnation." [20]

In 1974 Kristeva published *The revolution of poetic language,* the work in which she introduced the key concepts of the *semiotic* and the *symbolic*. In Lacan's theories of the 1930's a major emphasis was the elaboration of the symbolic order, which refers to the dimension of

---

[19] Anne-Marie Smith, *Language the Unknown: An initiation into Linguistics,* tr. Anne M. Menke (New York: Columbia University Press, 1998), p. 14.

[20] Kristeva, quoted in Smith, p. 32.

language. Later on Lacan established the parity and relevance of the other two areas: the Imaginary and the Real. Kristeva departs from Lacan to study the pre-verbal, *semiotic* stage and its manifestations in language or in the symbolic. This departure involves the study of the child's relationship with the mother prior to language. In psychoanalysis this stage is known as the pre-oedipal stage or the period of primary narcissism. The semiotic, as Kristeva uses the term, relates to corporeal memory, a reminiscence of the play of energy and drives experienced in the body before real and symbolic separation from the mother-- before we can talk about subjectivity. The symbolic, as with Lacan, refers to the establishment of sign and syntax, the paternal function, social constrains and the symbolic law [Law of the father].

Although Kristeva acknowledges the Freudian tradition that made manifest the structural importance of the Oedipus complex and of the phallus, she emphasizes also the forms of modification, transgression and revolt which take place before the law of that order. The study of this pre-oedipal stage is her contribution. Kristeva mentions that the human capacity to create sacred and symbolic meaning (including music) depends on this dimension of the pre-verbal, semiotic, archaic maternal space.

Kristeva's latest work involves further elaboration of the category of the semiotic and its interaction with the symbolic. For her, music, poetry, art and dance are codes-- practices that allow performers and artists as subjects to be at the same time both transgressive and contained by the social order. An example of this is the fact that it is socially accepted for any singer or instrumentalist to show aggressiveness, sensuality, body movements and a wide range of emotions that might not seem appropriate in other social contexts. Musicality is an expression of semiotic, unnamable forces and drives. Kristeva compares the interaction of the semiotic with the symbolic to the musicians and artists who need to attack or modify standard, traditional forms. Kristeva tells us, "since the subject is always both semiotic and symbolic any signifying system he/she produces is never 'exclusively' symbolic, but marked by a debt to the other modality."[21]

Activities such as performing or composing music have a close relation to the semiotic. For instance, avant-garde music could be conceived as an attempt to fracture the totalizing discourse of fixed perceptions (the symbolic world). However, the interaction with the symbolic is always present. No one altogether escapes tradition. Kristeva reminds us that although music might be thought to be exclusively semiotic, musicians must deal with symbolic codes, structures such as music notation or other cultural conventions, and must use language to talk about them.

Kristeva compares the composer of music, in touch with the chaos of drives and striving to give them form, with the mother, who must educate the infant driven by bodily needs, and also with the psychoanalyst, who provides a structure for the patient's regression to the memory of his childhood. We can associate the semiotic with the child's pre-verbal relationship with the mother's body, and the symbolic with language and separation from the mother. Music, conceived as an expression of the semiotic, seems to challenge the symbolic world: where language divides, music wishes to unite. For example, the sense of communion that we

---

[21] Kristeva, quoted in Smith, p. 19.

musicians all feel either performing or listening, involves an identification with something that is both inside and outside ourselves.

In order to elaborate on the dialectical relation between the symbolic and the semiotic, Kristeva invoked the concept of the *chora*. *Chora,* a term meaning receptacle, is a term borrowed from Plato who described it as "an invisible and formless being which receives all things and in some mysterious way partakes of the intelligible, and is most incomprehensible."[22] Plato used this notion to describe chaotic matter for creation of the universe. Kristeva used it in explaining the creation of the subject. As Smith explains it, "Kristeva introduces into her formulation of the semiotic the concept of a non-expressive in the sense of non-verbal totality underlying language; a non-spatial, non-temporal receptacle of energy and drives which she calls the chora." [23]

By introducing the semiotic, a supplementary third dimension into the lacanian model of the Imaginary and the Symbolic, Kristeva introduces a space occupied by sensation, sounds and images. Language *and* body memories are processes that define subjectivity. In this way, Kristeva claims to regain the body that was lost in Lacan's theories.

Kristeva's elaboration of the *chora* suggests an understanding of music as a form of human expression and communication somehow lying outside the world of language. She

---

[22] Plato, *Timaeus,* (tr. Jowett), *p. 51.*

[23] Smith, p. 21.

defined the semiotic "as musical, anterior, enigmatic, mysterious and rhythmic."[24] The *chora* is for her feminine, in the sense that it precedes any formation of subjectivity and phallic identity. It represents femininity in distinction to the masculinity of the symbolic order. Smith comments, "It is the mother who for the child, and metaphorically for culture at large, facilitates, enacts and embodies the passage between semiotic and symbolic modalities and the path to representation."[25]

The interaction between the semiotic and the symbolic remains present during our whole life. It is a struggle between the melancholy of the loss of the mother and the search for subjectivity in the symbolic (phallic) world. Kristeva sees musicians, poets and other artists as the best representatives of this struggle. Performance and musical composition occupy a "transitional and revolutionary space between abjection or confusion with the mother's body and too rigid identification with the symbolic father- or totalitarianism."[26] Music is a practice that seems to open the space for representing the Real or the unnamable. Just because we cannot articulate the meaning of music in words, it does not imply that music lacks meaning. Thus Kristeva has at least partially opened the door for the interpretation of music in her latest work, but unfortunately she has not gone through it into new territory.

In assessing Kristeva's importance, I agree with Shepherd and Wicke's comments,

---

[24] Kristeva, *The Revolution of Poetic Language* (Paris: Seuil 1974), p. 233.

[25] Smith, p. 22.

[26] Smith, p.38.

Considerable progress [in our understanding of music] has been made through our interrogation of French-language structuralism, semiology and psychoanalytic theory. The idea that music signifies through processes that are inherently structural in character has been lent credibility and strengthened through our consideration of the work of Saussure...Lacan and Kristeva...Considerable progress has also been made on the question of how music, as structural mode of signification, can impart its meaning to subjects. A direct material link between the sounds of music and the somatic pathways of the body has been posited in which the manner of connection circumvents the world of objects and the world of language. The positing of such a link is made possible through the work of Kristeva, building as it does, on the work of Lacan and Freud.[27]

---

[27] Shepherd and Wicke, p. 97

Preliminary Conclusions

It is not the purpose of this chapter to confront or debate Kristeva's views. I do, however, agree with Shepherd and Wicke that Kristeva's notion of a "different order of differences" in music has remained undeveloped. Kristeva leaves space to consider a possibility that many musicians already intuitively assume: that music conveys meaning. Many recent articles and books suggest a trend of theorists searching for a way to articulate an account of profundity, ineffability, or meaning in music.[28] This study deals mostly with the issue of subjectivity and music, with a clear awareness that further accounts of meaning in music would involve (in addition) a discussion of the social aspect of music and the inherent elements of music (timbre, harmony, rhythm, music history, performance practices, aesthetics etc.). I will discuss some of those issues in the third chapter.

Furthermore, Kristeva's theory of music offers intriguing possibilities for the development of the study of the body and gesture --both musical gesture and gesture in musical performance. By studying music as a practice with its own distinctive relation to the unconscious, psycho-sexual processes and the world of emotions, we gain new expertise in our role as performers, composers and listeners. For example, we could explore such questions as

---

[28] The list is vast. To name a few: Stanley Cavell, "Music Discomposed," in. *Must We Mean What We Say? A Book of Essays* (Cambridge and New York: Cambridge University Press, 1976); Jenefer Robinson, editor, *Music and Meaning*, (Ithaca: Cornell University Press, 1997); Aaron Ridley, *Music, Value, and the Passions* (Ithaca: Cornell University Press, 1995): Diana Raffman, *Language, Music, and Mind* (Cambridge, Mass. : MIT Press, 1993).

the following: Do the psychoanalytic concept of the Other, desire, and symbolic-semiotic dimensions help to explain meaningful musical performance? To what extent do Kristeva's psychoanalytic theories account for the nature of what has been called the sublime or contemplative in music? As we shall see, this line of thought will be continued in chapter II with Didier-Weill's work and in chapter III on the sublime and the performing experience.

To summarize briefly, with her emphasis on the mother-infant relation, Kristeva brings attention to the pre-oedipal, semiotic stage--which is the stage of physicality and emotion. This stage continues to exist within us during our whole life, and through music we get in touch with it. This is the place that allows for unnamable, non-verbal, and deep emotional forms of expression.

CHAPTER II:

Didier-Weill and Music as an Expression of a Drive.

Let us now proceed to discuss music and meaning. In this chapter I will focus on discussing music from the standpoint of psychoanalysis. I find these theories insightful and helpful to understand our relation with music, whether we are listeners, performers or composers.

I have always thought that conventional music analysis, whether it is harmonic, formal, or counterpoint analysis, never satisfactorily addresses the question of why music affects us so profoundly. Why does music like Rachmaninov's cello sonata in G Minor to name one example, engage us so emotionally that all of a sudden while listening or performing it, we might think: "What is happening to me?" Why are my emotions are so powerful that and I have the sensation of going to another world?"

There have been around one hundred years of different theories about emotion. Since the work of Sigmund Freud, the father of psychoanalysis, we know that human beings have drives in a fundamental quest to be satisfied. Freud defined the drive as a concept on the borders between the body and the mind. The difference from an instinct is that to one instinct corresponds one object (as in the case of hunger-food) while the drive can be satisfied by a variety of objects. There is also, a dimension of our lives that we don't know about it, our unconscious being. His practice revealed that we all have a quest to satisfy needs that are not biological but psychological. Thus, Freud spoke of objects of a drive, for example the oral, the anal, and the genital.

It was Jacques Lacan who later identified the voice (the sound) and the gaze as objects of a drive. Lacan is famous for his statement that our unconscious is structured like a language. Since for many of us music is the "language" of our lives, it seems justified to pursue this exploration of psychoanalytic terrain. If nothing else, it might shed light on our relationship with music.

Lacan also said that human cultural life culture develops in three zones: (1) the Symbolic (language, the law which Lacan referred to as the law of the father), (2) the Imaginary (our fantasies, conscious or unconscious) and (3) the Real, which is what exists and cannot be named. Reality for Lacan includes the things we agree upon and have been established. The Rachmaninov cello sonata, for example, exhibits the three Lacanian levels. The Imaginary involves the sounds, images, etc., that Rachmaninov initially conceived. The Symbolic world in music is represented by our agreement about intonation, musical writing, and performing tradition. The Real is the meaning that the music conveys which cannot be translated into words. Thus the Real is that which is outside language, resisting symbolization absolutely.

Freud and Lacan tell us that we have undergone a loss in our process of being incorporated into the world of language and that our life is marked with that lack. As Lacan said: "all forms of Art are characterized by a certain mode of organization around [a] void."[29] Lacan's works have opened a path for his followers to study the arts.

Lacan's disciple Alain Didier-Weill is one of the current psychoanalysts that continue to develop Lacan's theories. He is a frequent lecturer in psychoanalytic conventions in Europe and the US. Didier-Weill is currently one of the directors of the New York Psychoanalytic school *"Apres-Coup"*. In his works, he explores diverse aspects of the relationship of psychoanalysis with music, dance, drama and art.

Didier-Weill is also a playwright author. He studied psychoanalysis with Lacan and was his assistant. He is member of *l' Ecole Freudienne*, cofounder of the movement *Coup Freudienne* and president of the movement *Insistance*. He has many years of clinical practice as a psychoanalyst and is professor of psychoanalysis in the University of Paris VII. He has published several books, articles and numerous theater productions. Among his most famous psychoanalytic works are: *Les Trois Temps de la Loi* (Seuil, 1996), *Invocations* (Calmann-Levy, 1998) and *Quartier Lacan* (Denoel, 2001).

In December of 1976 Lacan asked Didier- Weill to participate in one of the lectures of his last seminar (still not published). After his participation, Lacan asked Didier-Weill to organize his exposition and publish it. According to Lacan, Didier-Weill established the basis to analyze music or the musical experience as a way to account for the existence of the "invocative drive[30]" (*la pulsion invoquante*). Soon after this, Didier-Weill published in the magazine *Ornicar*

---

[29] Jacques Lacan, *Seminary VII: The Ethics of Psychoanalysis*, p.155.

[30] For a reference about the subject and the drives see Lacan: *The Four fundamentals concepts of Psychoanalysis*.

an article titled: "De quatre temps subjectivants dans la musique." Here he developed his concept of the "Blue note", a concept he considered a second contribution to the problem of the invocative drive.

These two contributions, the invocative drive and the Blue note, are the issues that I propose to investigate in the present study. They are major points of the psychoanalytic work in Didier-Weill's investigations. It is inside of these theories of subjectivity that we will develop a discussion of music as an "Other" to whom we listen and by whom we are listened. This will also account for an investigation about music and meaning, and the power of music to create emotional response from us.

Let us start by observing that when psychoanalysis speaks of the voice or sound (referred to as "the invocative drive"), it refers to a process by which the sound is constituted in each individual as an object of a drive. The object is lost from the very outset and independent of any reference to a tangible object of "reality" in the way the term is usually understood. These theories of Freud and the French school of psychoanalysis I present here are relevant because music is considered as the sound that occupies a fundamental place in the structure of any subject[31] or human foundation. Another fundamental claim in these theories is that our existence is structured in a dialectical relationship with the Other. [32] Instead of "I think

---

[31] I use the term subject throughout this study as referred in psychoanalytic terms: the individual with his/her unconscious.

[32] As Lacan defines the subject: "... If the subject is defined by language and the words, this means that the subject, in initio, begins in the place of the Other, since that is the place where the first significant arises", *The Four Fundamental concepts of Psychoanalysis*, p. 206

therefore I exist" they state "I am listened then I exist". Our life is determined by the existence of this Other to whom we address demands things and from whom we also receive demands.

So for the psychoanalysts something occurs with the sound or invocative drive. But how exactly does this drive originate? [33]Psychoanalysis reconstructs the mythical moment by a postulate based on what has been observed and analyzed. It goes like this: at the beginning of his life the infant (like every human and unlike animals entirely dependent upon the Other for the satisfaction of his needs) gives out a cry. It does not matter if it is literally the first cry or not. What matters is that this cry is a pure expression through sound (the voice) associated with a state of internal displeasure and that this cry is answered by the Other (usually the mother). The mother or other person attributes meaning to this cry, interpreting it as hunger, thirst, etc., and brings to the child something that calms down the tension, something that can be considered a first satisfaction. A trace of this satisfaction will remain in the child's memory and will be associated with certain elements: physical contact, feeding, a sonorous stimulation, etc. The child will also acquire a representation of first *jouissance*[34].

These memory traces will also be associated with the sonority of his cry. This cry is not a priori a call, much less a demand. It is just a simple expression of discomfort. It is the Other who, in attributing meaning to the cry, raises it to the status of a demand. By doing so, the mother also inscribes it with the mark of her own desire ("what does my baby want?"). This first

---

[33] Here I paraphrase some arguments used in Michel Poizat, *The Blue Note, and The Objectified Voice and the Vocal Object*, (Cambridge University Press, 1991), pp. 195-211

[34] The French word *jouissance* means approximately enjoyment, but it has a sexual connotation (i.e. 'orgasm') lacking in the English word enjoyment, and is therefore left without translation in most English editions of Lacan.

cry is hypothetical because as soon it is interpreted, its "purity" is lost forever. The purity of the sound is now caught in the web of signification that occurs with the intervention of the Other.

Then comes a second phase, when the baby cries again. With this second cry everything is different. The sound is a call for somebody or for something. It is not a "pure" sound but an invocation. This time the cry is no longer a sound. Instead it acquires the status of a demand, a demand for the return of the object of the first enjoyment. Thus the cry now acquires the status of language and meaning. Whatever the mother does to calm the baby is never identical to the first time, so the first object of *jouissance* is irremediably lost.

The sound that took part in the first *jouissance* can be the sound of the voice of the baby or the mother. The important thing here is that is a sound. The search for a sound is understood, then, as an attempt to recover a sonorous materiality that is already lost. From the second phase on, the cry exists only as a demand. In other words, *the sound is produced to cause an effect* that the mother will interpret and react to. This interaction with the Other is our access to language. The cry has a meaning. However, the sound, the particularities of the cry, becomes a lost *jouissance*. Lacan called this a place of nothingness, as a representation for that loss. It is in this framework, namely, the relation of the child with the Other as it was described above, that the whole relationship with language is established. Our relationship with music is that lost *jouissance*. That is the place where we find the happiness once lost, which we again find through music.

The sound is something that surrounds us. First, there is a tension between sound and meaning: sound can even undermine meaning. One example could be my accent when speaking English. Maybe my accent, apart from the meaning of what I am saying when I speak evokes my ethnicity, culture and its values. My accent also brings the sound, the materiality of sound as an intrusion into English, subverting the signification of the spoken words. When this happens, when the sound subverts the meaning, our relationship with the materiality of sound becomes an object of *jouissance*. The sound as an object is understood as a lost object like the very first object of *jouissance*. The conclusion is that sound, including music, involves a quest for the lost object, a search for a lost sonorous materiality, now dissolved beyond signification.

This could explain how music, for musicians and listeners, has a powerful meaning and at the same time exceeds the meaning as expressed in language. You can have many different images about Rachmaninov's music: and all of them can be truthful representations of his music. Music is something that we cannot categorize. Music provokes such powerful emotions that it makes us wonder "What is happening to me?"

One important point I would like to make in this chapter is that one reason for these emotional upheavals resides in music' destruction of meaning. Music brings a reencounter with a Real that has been excluded from us. We performers all know how the voice of our instrument touches us so deeply. For example, someone who listened to Maria Callas was once asked if he was crying because he knew she is going to kill herself. He replied "No, it was the sound of her voice". Many times my cello teacher has made a similar observation: that the answer to a problematic passage is simply to let the music answer it. Many famous musicians have embraced the same position: that the most valuable knowledge we have about music is intuitive, is the result of our talent to listen the message that music transmits.

Didier-Weill tells us that music "transmits a significant without signifier. Music does not require a time to translate its meaning. In this point lies the fundamental difference between a word and a note of music."[35] He adds that the fact that music can transmit a significant message without a signifier (without a univocal meaning) implies that this message cuts the circuit of words and their representations to address the representation of the invocative drive.[36] To put in his words, Didier-Weill explains that without the thinking structure of language, music creates an "otherness" which directly affects the Real that the drive source represents. Let us try to clarify this point.

A Contribution to the Question of the Invocative Drive

In order to study music and the subject, Didier-Weill refers to the invocative drive. This drive has different stages that are not chronological but logical. He begins with the fact that we are "touched" by the music. It is as if, thanks to the music, we receive a certain response. Didier-Weill states that, "The problem starts by stating the fact that this response that music arouses in us bring out in us a precedent question that we had and we did not know that we had".[37] Music represents then an "otherness"[38] that listens to something in us that we did not

---

[35] Alain Didier-Weill, *Lila et la lumiere de Vermeer*, (Paris: editions Denoel 2003), p. 44.
[36] Freud had established the basic definition of the drives. With Lacan we have four: the oral, anal, the gaze and the voice. The invocative drive is an elaboration of the implications of the drive of the voice. The drives are partial in the sense that they are not the end of biological reproduction but rather to satisfy a need partially.

[37] Didier-Weill, as cited above, p. 137.
[38] As Lacan defines the subject: "... If the subject is defined by language and the words, this means that the subject, in initio, begins in the place of the Other, since that is the place where the first significant arises". *The Four Fundamental concepts of Psychoanalysis*. P . 206

understand. In this regard we can consider that the first stage is music that "listens" to us rather than the opposite. For Didier-Weill, music "tell us" or "lets us see" the lack[39] that our being has. He states that one way to understand the essence of the movement of the drive(s) is to be aware that the subject is moved by the revelation of the existence of a [structural] lack, a nothingness, a void sustained by what Lacan has called the "object a."[40]

One problem that arises when considering music as the Other is to determine whether we are listening to the desire of the music itself or the desire of the Other. To be listening to the desire of the Other (personified in the music) seems unlikely to Didier-Weill, because the desire of the Other usually takes the form of a command, something that has a paralyzing effect on us. "What does she wants from me?" is the typical question-example, where not knowing what is expected from us or what we really want has a disquieting connotation. But to the contrary, music has a liberating effect on us; music imposes on us an unquestionable "Yes" as our response. This "Yes" represents the invocative drive. In music we find an "Other" that is not so foreign. The simplicity of this "Yes" does not mean that we understand it: our response, our "Yes" without questioning, is beyond our comprehension.

Didier-Weill presents this process as involving three stages of the drive: in the first stage of the drive, it is music that finds a receptive subject. This subject finds in the music a call for a lack that he did not know he has. This is called a subjective transmutation: a subject *listener* is

---

[39] Lacan established four different drives: the oral, anal, the gaze and the invocative drive which would be the voice. Our psycho-sexuality, a supplement to the biological sexuality to procreate, is the result of the interplay of the drives, which are only partial drives. "The drive is the structure through which sexuality participates in the psychic-life in a way that has to accommodate to the structure of lack that the unconscious has."

[40] In the psychoanalytic theory of Lacan, object a stands for the unattainable object of desire. It is sometimes called the object cause of desire.

transmuted into a subject *listened* to. If music has a particular relationship with the invocative drive-- according to Lacan-- the "closest to the experience of the unconscious", it lies in the fact that by the Yes we say, in response to music, a part of our *unconscious* self comes into existence. In other words, since music is something exterior to us, we depart from the Freudian conception of a discontinuity or separation between our interior self and the exterior world. Instead we are revealed, like the Moebian conception, to have continuity between the interior and exterior of our being.[41] Performing music is an experience of the "Other" as somebody not so foreign to us. In every phrase we play we try to recreate a music that is an expression of Rachmaninov as much as it is of ourselves.

Didier-Weill says that the second stage happens when the notes that were addressed in the first stage from the Other (the music) to the subject (us) becomes a return of the drive in the opposite direction, from the subject to the Other. This is the moment in which we understand the structure of the music but also reach a point of hallucinating that we are the composer. It is a point where the notes we perform or listen to seem to be ours. It is as if it was I who created the melody I am playing or belonged to me from before. The emotion and understanding that music creates has no need for language or any symbolic system to mediate. It evokes an immediate response from us. The sadness or melancholy that a work of Rachmaninoff expresses is "our" sadness or melancholy.

In many cases we anticipate a harmony or melodic gesture. Though the question of structure and design has other elements to consider that I will refer to later on, the question of

---

[41] Lacan called that with a neologism: the "ex-time".

the union between the performer or listener and the composer is the point I would like to stress here. This confusion (or hallucination, as Didier-Weill referred to it), resembles a type of "madness" that we commonly refer to as Love[42]. Our practice, study, and constant attempts to improve our expressive musical skills are the result of a Yes that has to do with love. This is like love understood as music listening to us; it reveals a lack, a dimension of our being that somehow turns us into lovers of music. This is a crucial point since the musician and the mystic would have something in common: they both, rather than loving the Other, *respond* to the love of the Other.

In this view, there is no fusion between the I and the Other. According to Didier-Weill, Freud misunderstood this distinction when he referred to the musical experience as the "oceanic feeling", a regression to the mother, or archaic fusion. That music can be conceived as an expression of a drive is because it presents a tension, a drive movement. Didier-Weill concludes that this similarity of the subject with the Other arouses a "hope" of identity [or fusion]. When the subject does not find it, instead of being hopeless, he creates a new way to renew the hope: he will not wait for the Other but will go towards the Other, he will go to listen, to perform, to compose.

It is important to clarify the notion of the lack that music reveals in us. For Didier-Weill, this lack is not the cause of sadness, but nostalgia. Music has this nostalgic dimension regardless of the character of the music. It is a nostalgia we feel as a result of this lack that is structural in our being, in our lives. Perhaps this is one of the reasons we enjoy sad music.

---

[42] Didier-Weill establishes a parallel with the two stages that Lacan discuss in his seminary about the Transference as necessary for love to occurs.

However, Didier-Weill cites Victor Hugo, who proclaimed that nostalgia is the opposite of being sad. Hugo seems to have an insight into this "well-being," a nice feeling that nostalgia brings to us: It is not only the acknowledgement of our lack, a renouncing of the object we once loved, but also a feeling of well-being that comes from living with this experience of lack.

Finally, Didier-Weill argues that there is a third stage after the subject realizes the impossibility of finding the object that the Other lacks, or the object that the subject lacks. In this stage, the subject is able to relate to the lack on both sides, that of the subject and of the Other. Didier-Weill concludes that music rather than being a sublimation of a sexual drive is more the expression of an experience of the sublime.

The Blue Note

What is the power of music that transports us from one place to another? To answer this question, Didier-Weill maintains that music provokes an emotion that has two movements or two states of mind simultaneously: a feeling of well-being and a state of nostalgia. We can neither measure nor understand the nature of this "nostalgic joy" [*jouissance*] that will arise in the instant that a note is played. This note is never monotonous even though it is always the same note. As one composer said once in lecture, "We spend our life composing and recomposing the same piece."[43] Any note, from any type of music, can became that note that Didier-Weill calls "The Blue Note," inspired by Delacroix's painting of a *Blue Note* while listening to Chopin's playing.

---

[43] Dr. James Mobberly, one of my compositions teachers at the Composers Seminar, University of Missouri Kansas City, Conservatory of Music.

In most of Western music we musicians, composers, and listeners are familiar with the binary structure of tension-release. This can be applied to different types and styles of music. I will refer to examples from my own experience. In the slow movement of the Rachmaninov cello sonata, we can see how every phrase is based on the tension between the harmony and the melody. We listen with increased emotion and tension because we have the hope of reaching that note that will resolve and give meaning to the phrase. That note is an example of the Blue Note. As a performer, it is the music that tells me, with its particular structure, the moment of arrival of this note. If I hold or try to possess this note at my will, I usually end up destroying the effect.

In performing music, the experience belongs to the ineffable. I can say that my body, my soul and my instrument are engaged in an experience of expression beyond any reasoning. In an effort to make sense of both concepts, the invocative drive and the Blue Note, I can summarize by saying that my body and myself, with my unconscious being, are engaged in an enthusiastic enjoyment of a Dionysian present that at the same time is a "becoming" of a forward movement. Toward where? Didier- Weill's answer is, toward the Blue Note.

The existence of the Blue Note is beyond any knowledge because this point is the "cause"[44] of the subject. As long as this "cause" is unconscious we also remain unconscious of its "cause". Our access to that point is represented by a forward movement, a drive. When performing music, our bodily movement and production of sound involve meaning because they answer to a call, an invocation towards an indefinite future. Music is a hope that waiting

---

[44] The cause of the subject is according to Freud the primordial repression, becoming foreclosure, that the subject experiences.

for that future is not in vain. For psychoanalysis it is important to know that the cause of this Blue Note is in the repressed, lost past of the individual in such a way that the individual through music can recover it and say without mistake, "I am going toward the Blue Note."

Music and Time

For musicians it is a revealing concept that the world we inhabit when listening, performing or composing music is a world not limited for the space-time received by the symbolic law [symbolic world]. Music allows us to go from measured time into absolute time. In our daily world, the present goes into the future in every moment. In music, understood as a dimension of absolute time, the rhythm aspect reminding us of the present moment and the hope of arrival of the Blue Note in the future are happening at the same time. Whenever we start to play music, the Blue Note, in spite of being absent, is symbolically present for me. In structuralist terms, the effect of the Blue Note is not in my doing but happens as a result of the fact that I am a subject. This note, Didier-Weill tells us, presents a structural character: for the unconscious is always the same. In spite of this, this note has the power of preventing monotony or boredom because of the enjoyment and "enchantment" it provokes. It does this as long as we keep in the present waiting for next note to come. This note has a special quality: it is offered to us in the moment we listen to it, the moment we play it, and at the same time, it escapes from us. For Didier-Weill this impossibility of possessing the note makes us become "possessed" by it. We cannot symbolize this note, nor retain the effect that it produces on us.

The fleetingness of the note in an instant reveals a secret "present" for us, namely: the present moment.

I think music presents also a particular temporal dimension. While it is possible to admire a sculpture or a painting for several minutes or hours, the performance of a musical work has a definite beginning and ending. Its existence last the performance time, at least for the aesthetic experience. Music presents then a clear analogy with life and death expressed in sound and silence. The meaning that the Blue Note conveys for us can create a sense of absolute time. The past, the present and the future combined in a note that reveals the potentiality of an instant.

Preliminary Conclusions

...music itself [is] the supreme mystery of the science of man, a mystery that all the various disciplines come up against and which holds the key to their progress". C. Levi-Strauss

    I think now we are in a position to give new insight into our definition of the invocative drive. The invocative drive should be understood as a feeling of going toward that signifier which is the holder of the ineffable—of what is beyond any specifiable significance. Didier-Weill makes us realize how composers and performers are the ones that are in a position of creating and revealing to us the ineffable, bringing back to us a sound that was previously excluded from the Real. Many poets have spoken metaphorically of a prison that they had to break out of in order to make the ineffable hearable. If they had to escape a symbolic code, is because that code (or symbolic agreement) is not suitable to represent what is ineffable.

    A point I would like to make is that when Didier-Weill, as well as other French psychoanalysts and philosophers, state that music, as opposed to language, has neither meaning nor finality, they refer to their view of music in which it exceeds the sense found in language. This implies that music can undermine the hierarchical binary structure of language. Didier-Weill emphasizes that music conveys a Real, a truth superior to language and at the same time it is incapable of being translatable into words. The attempt to translate a musical work into a univocal reference or meaning is in direct conflict with the work itself. Under this light, our inherited epistemological view is just one possible way to conceive the musical meaning of a work.

What I considered so far is in line with our discussion of music and its significance. While I do agree with Didier-Weill, I would like to mention that for many performers there are different levels of experiencing musical meaning. These levels come not only from our unconscious relation with music, reviving a pre-oedipal time, but also with something that the *object* imposes on us. Music conveys a paradoxical discourse. The relation of the subject with the object (music) is the topic for the third chapter.

Didier-Weill's insight is concerned with structure of the *subject*. Still, I think his contribution is most relevant for musicians as well as for psychoanalysts, philosophers and other people interested in exploring our relationship with music. His theory also leaves space to consider music on another "existential" level common to all of us. For example, the Blue Note in music is considered by Levi-Strauss as a point of "zero significance". In other words, the Blue Note has multiple significances-- as many meanings as there are individuals who listen to it. It offers to us all meanings or none, but in this way, under the impact of the Blue Note, everything acquires sense. The signifiers of the unconscious chain come into play, giving us a sense that the world "speaks" to us. For the person in love the world makes sense, may be because in the person loved just as in the Blue Note, there is a power to symbolize a limit while promising the unlimited. The limit in music is the limit of our senses and those sounds that are not yet hearable.

The fact that the Blue Note is expected does not mean that it does not surprise the audience. The Blue Note does not provoke *jouissance* only. Music's discourse or route toward the Blue Note is a preliminary pleasure, as in love's prelude of foreplay. It has the connotation of a promise of pleasure. For Didier-Weill, what happens in the instant we hear the Blue Note involves the dialectic of the subject and the Other. In this moment, we are, as Didier-Weill puts it, "neither one nor the Other." Didier-Weill's thesis, which I would like to extend also to the performer, is this: "The listener [and the performer] of music are simultaneously the one and the Other."

At first when performing or listening to music, we are in the terrain of the Other. If certain music appeals to us, or moves us, it is because that music offers a response to a question that we already had. It is as if the Other (the performer for the audience, the composer for the performer) has listened to our call (the invocative drive). The discovery that music reveals in us dimensions that we did not know allows us to question whether music *reveals or creates* the divided subject. The magic appeal of the Blue Note is that it facilitates the encounter with the Other in a point common to both (subject and the Other): what Lacan would call *the object a*. The subject and music as the Other recognize each other through what they do not have.

When we perform a piece, say a Bach Prelude for example, we can express the architecture of the piece knowing that music is never a consummated thing but always in the process of "becoming". The meaning we attribute to it is not at the beginning of the phrase but is rather the realization of a promise we put into the music beforehand. Didier-Weill says that the task of the performer is to play music in a way that allows the audience to "abolish themselves" as an Other totally different from the performer. Didier-Weill says that the performer and the audience have a tacit agreement. It is as if the performer says to the audience: You have to right to expect from me this which I find and make you also realize its existence: the Blue Note.

My cello teacher used to say that a more precise word than performer is 'co-creator', since it is our responsibility to express something exterior to us but that is a part of ourselves when performing. With Didier-Weill's insight, we performers can create a discourse that conveys the particularity of a hope, an expectation, in other words a realization of a promise that could be just that chord, that note, or that dynamic point. In the search for the Blue Note, the performer is a co-creator.

CHAPTER III:

From the Subject to the Music

So far I have presented what music represents for an individual, a subject, in psychoanalytic terms. In chapter I, Kristeva's concepts enabled us to develop an account of music as a drive, opening the door for us to think about music, the sublime and the meaning of music.

In Chapter II, with Didier-Weill, we saw music in relation to a "subject", considering music, sound and its relevance to our human constitution. I presented questions such as: Why is it that so many times when we perform, we feel as if we were transported by music to other places? Didier-Weill describes music as the expression of a drive, namely, the invocative drive. He also concludes that music rather than being a sublimation of a sexual drive is more the expression of an experience of the sublime.

However, Kristeva and Didier-Weill do not focus on music as an object of study, rather on the subject of the unconscious. In order to develop a thesis relevant for musicians it is necessary to establish a common ground between psychoanalysis and aesthetics. One of the reasons for the study of the psychoanalytic field is that that I am trying to convey a truth, aware that any "authentic" truth would come from a subject that is existentially engaged, affected by the enunciation of such a truth. To disregard the subject of the enunciation would constitute an inauthentic knowledge. For example, I find many approaches and analyses of music by music theorists are attempts to find universals. What I have in mind is, say, the attempt to study and analyze a Bach choral, or a Rachmaninov prelude, the way scientists analyze the spectrum of a distant star. I would certainly agree that we can find common practices, even universal practices in many music periods. However these practices may be the expression of what composers and performers felt should be universal.

Instead, I propose for the performer to be aware of our constitution as a subject of the unconscious when performing or composing music. In other words, I propose a quest not toward the absolute truth, concerning the meaning of music, in our condition of human speakers and musicians, but a quest for a *little more truth*. Also, our expression and findings in music, what we express or find meaningful to highlight in a performance, "reveals us" to a certain extent. We are revealed in our performance choices and movements. But that does not drain off the river of this investigation. Music is not just about you or me as a subject. A work of art is there and our relationship with it is the topic of this third chapter.

Didier Weill helps us to understand that truth and knowledge are related as desire is related with drive. In psychoanalysis, the aim of the therapist is through the treatment, "through the talking cure", to (re) focus attention to progress to a new knowledge which dwells at the place of truth. This is a notion of truth that reflects a philosophical tradition from Kierkegaard to Heidegger of despising mere "factual truth". In fact, Lacan himself in the 1960s focused his attention on drive, as a kind of "acephalic" knowledge which brings about satisfaction. Slavoj Zizek, in his article "Desire: Drive=Truth: Knowledge", relates this drive for knowledge to the practice of modern scientists,

> Modern Science follows its path (in microbiology, in manipulating genes, etc.), heedless of cost, satisfaction is here provided by knowledge itself, not by any moral or communal goals scientific knowledge is supposed to serve....the notion of re-inscribing scientific drive into the constraint of the life-world is

fantasy at it purest, perhaps the fundamental fascist fantasy.[45]

I have showed in this study that our experience of music is related to a drive. I will also explore the musical experience as an opportunity to access another "mode of being", beyond ethics, beyond reason and common sense, beyond the symbolic world. In other words, I propose an exploration of aesthetics, and the need for a new aesthetic, one with different approaches to conceive musical meaning which will unfold from the study of music and the experience of the sublime. Finally, I will make some suggestion on the musical experience in light of our previous considerations.

Let us proceed then to a discussion about music. In order to investigate meaning and music, it is necessary now to address the object music. This object, to which we dedicate a great amount of time in our life, has an existence beyond ourselves, beyond the individual. For the purpose of this investigation I will try to define the object "music" to which I will refer. First, the word "music" refers to a wide spectrum of sounds and circumstances. Music can be the sound (or silence) that an expectant audience produces before a pianist who remains silent, without playing, as in the conception of John Cage's piece 4'33". Or the sound of a butterfly freed in front of a microphone, as in one of the compositions of Morton Feldman. Music can be the repetitive rhythm of a percussion instrument accompanying a dancer toward the ecstasy honoring the Bacchic gods or the percussive electronic rhythm in a night club for dancers in a search of erotic ecstasy.

In this work I refer to music as an art form, music conceived with listeners in mind in a

---

[45] Slavoj Zizek, "Desire: Drive= Truth: Knowledge." UMBR(a). Center for the Study of Psychoanalysis and Culture, SUNY Buffalo, 2005, p. 2.

theater or a chamber room. In particular, instrumental music, music without words, absolute music. Carl Dalhaus tells us that absolute music is historically rooted in the idea of an unspeakable sublime, in the idea that "music expresses what words are not even capable of stammering"[46]. As a performer, to follow the line of thought of Kristeva and Didier-Weill, I have no doubt that on occasion performing, composing or listening to some Western music is an experience of the sublime. Why are the performance and the study of music so meaningful for many of us?

Discussing music and meaning for many authors means discussing emotion. It is clear that music moves us in many ways. The concept of music arousing emotions is a very old idea dating back to Plato, Pythagoras, etc. During the seventeenth and eighteenth centuries the rhetorical tradition in music emphasized the arousal of "affects" as a main goal of music. In the Baroque period, the use of certain affects such as love, joy, or sadness gave a principle of unity for constructing a piece. Bach's cello suites are an example where we could easily identify this principle of construction. Thus we can appreciate this in the "youthful" suite in G major, the "obscure and sad" suite in D minor or the "triumphal" suite in C major, etc. This idea continued to be used in Classicism. For example, Haydn stated that a composer was a craftsman whose job is to arouse sentiments. In the Romantic period the composer was supposed to communicate to an audience so that the listeners could recreate these emotions in their own experience. For many colleagues, professors and artists I have consulted and read, this idea is not only still prevalent but also a truthful description of the performing experience.

In the last 150 years of musical aesthetics, many theorists advocated and privileged the

---

[46] Carl Dahlhaus, *The idea of Absolute Music*, tr. Roger Lustig, (University of Chicago Press, 1989), p.63.

idea of autonomous musical meaning. To summarize this view I will examine ideas of Eduard Hanslick, the founder of formalist musical aesthetics; Peter Kivy, a well-known modern representative of formalism; and, opposed to them, Jenefer Robinson, a philosopher, who has presented a theory of emotions.

Philosophers address the question of whether music moves us through the emotions it contains or causes or through something else. Eduard Hanslick denied that music moves us by virtue of its emotive content. According to him, emotions involve definitive referential thoughts such as fear or sadness about something or someone. What is beautiful and meaningful about music, according to Hanslick, is essentially musical in character. Its value consists in the autonomous beauty of forms moving tonally, the musical elements of construction (melody, harmony, rhythm, timbre, etc.) out of which music is composed. Hanslick also stressed the point that the meaning of music cannot be put into words. A composition does not start out as concepts which the composer then transforms into tones. Rather, it is tones themselves that are the starting point for the musical work. Since music belongs to the ineffable, it is only possible to give an intuitive approach regarding the meaning in which the musical elements have been combined in the piece.

In spite of his rejection of extra-musical reference, Hanslick as a critic, on many occasions explained music outside the scope that he suggested in his theories. For instance, he describes the first movement of Brahms's symphony No 1 as a "dark Faustian struggle... of a suffering abnormally agitated individual."[47] He explained this fact by stating that it is possible to

---

[47] Eduard Hanslick, *Vom Musikalisch-Schonen (On the Musically Beutiful)*, tr. Geoffrey Payzant, (Indianapolis: Hackett Publishing Company, 1986), p. 5.

use metaphorical language to describe music provided that we do not take the description seriously. This view presents the controversial conclusion that musical meaning is not only inarticulate but also invariant. The music itself guards the identity of the work, the conception of an invariant trace, recognizably the same for all listeners in a given culture. There may be cultural filters through which people can hear musical meaning. This particular piece can be interpreted like this by one culture, like that by another.

One might say that this very invariance is a product of representational practices and of attitudes towards representation. This view sees an unproblematic and self-evident isomorphism between score and work. This very invariance is the product of a construction of music in terms of works as ontologically stable entities.

Hanslick's view is in clear tension with a more historically focused conception of music, which suggests a more interactive process. Rather than seeing music as a reified, trans-historical entity, the historical view considers music within the musical community for which it was initially produced. Our previous psychoanalytic investigation seems to be closer to this latter position. For psychoanalysis human beings are the producers and the product of a culture. Language and sound are instances that precede the individual. In most musical circles this view is accepted as truth; we acknowledge that questions about musical meaning have different answers in different times, for different people, within different schools. Musical truth is not something timeless and univocal, but historically grounded.

I affirm in this work that music can be both things at the same time: both univocal and relative. But in order to claim this we need a revision of the concept of meaning as well as a new aesthetics, a new regimen of the sensible. This new aesthetics is one that offers us insight into the paradoxes of musical discourse. It is quite clear that any musical work is related to a history and to an individual who also has a history, a taste and a school of performance. At the same time, following Didier-Weill, if music is a revelation of a drive, something from a mythical moment before language, and something timeless, that has a place in our human constitution, we might ask ourselves: "Can music convey something that has relevance beyond time and place—express something from life itself? Can music add an "existential" quality of being that is universal?

Before I go further into these questions let us examine the other authors. In *Music Alone,* Kivy presents new arguments for the claim that meaningful instrumental music depends on the content alone. Kivy does not deny that instrumental music can express emotion. However, he says that the emotions one finds in the music of Brahms, for example, are phenomenal properties relating to nothing other that the music itself. He nevertheless accepts within musical phenomenological content properties that are *interpretable* in extra-musical terms. He includes not only dynamics of emotion, but the emotions themselves, the "garden variety", such as emotions of joy, sadness, etc.

Kivy establishes an important distinction regarding musical meaning and musical interpretation. As Patricia Herzog explains in her article, "Music Criticism and Musical Meaning"[48], "what music can mean differs from what it does mean." Kivy's distinction between musical meaning and music interpretation represents a significant departure from Hanslick's theory of musical meaning. Even though for both authors music means something that is exclusively musical, the properties of music for Kivy are much broader than for Hanslick. What can be a metaphor or figurative speech for Hanslick is for Kivy something that can be literally applied to the meaning of a piece.

---

[48] Patricia Herzog, "Music Criticism and Musical Meaning", *The Journal of Aesthetics and Art Criticism*, Summer 1995, 53:3.

In this way, Kivy opens the door for extra-musical considerations to come into play. Kivy's formalism seems better expressed by his claim that the extra-musical interpretation of musical content is by and large aesthetically irrelevant. His definition of music is "quasi-syntactic structure of musical properties, some of which are described in phenomenological terms."[49] He likens the "quasi-syntactic structure" of music to a semantically interpreted system of signs.[50] Thus, music, as in symbolic logic operations, has a structure governed by the rules of the composition. Interpretation then would be irrelevant because when a form of reasoning is valid, it is valid under any circumstances—univocal, we could say.

In his book *Sound and Semblance*, Kivy discusses at length the question of a valid interpretation,

> For, it might be argued, in defending the representational powers of music, have I not opened the door again to those infernal asses who must find a story in Beethoven's piano sonatas, and pictures in the Well-Tempered Clavier, and to those teachers, devoid of all musical intelligence, who impart 'musical appreciation' to their young prisoners by encouraging them to freely associate as a substitute for listening, thus transforming Beethoven's Fifth Symphony into Rorschach's First?[51]

Kivy proceeds then to prevent this by linking interpretation to the activity of problem-solving,

> in music, we are driven to seek a representational or pictorial answer to a problem in those instances where, for one thing, a purely musical one will not suffice...In short, interpretation removes the perplexity which gave rise to it without leaving any others to resolve in its place. It satisfies.[52]

To illustrate this problem, Kivy gives the example of Bach's Prelude in C Minor from the first

---

[49] Peter Kivy, *Music Alone*. (Cornell University Press, 1990) p.196

[50] Ibid., p. 196.

[51] Peter Kivy, *Sound and Semblance*, (Cornell University Press, 1984 and 1991), p. 197.
[52] Ibid., pp. 206-207.

book of the Well-Tempered Clavier. In referring to this piece he gives an "autumnal" interpretation, "the rustling sixteenth- notes figure, in both the right and left hands, that pervades the entire piece, represents the rustling of the dry autumn leaves in the cold October wind."[53] For Kivy, while some features of Bach's music could be described and related to autumn and leaves, such an interpretation is aesthetically irrelevant. Why? Because there is no puzzle that this interpretation solves, no "facts" about the music that it explains.

I can understand Kivy's attempt to preserve music from the hegemony of language. Most performers I know like to discuss music in musical terms. What is relevant is the meaning we find departing from musical experience and musical analysis. Or at least that is what we think we do. Perhaps this is the point when Kivy addresses the listener who obtains pleasure from absolute music without needing free associations: "There is no need to appeal to drunken orgies, heroes, or Faustian conflicts to experience the best of Beethoven, or Brahms symphonies." However, in spite of his position, I wonder to what extent the meaning of music is exhausted by the musical understanding we have of the work. Is the work or the emotions the work arouses in us the powerful meaning of music? Is it there something else?

Jenefer Robinson in her book *Deeper than Reason* raises questions such as "What is expression? How music does achieve expression? Or what are the grounds of artistic expression?" Her answers will come from a theory of emotion. Emotion, as she says, is "not a state but a process, an interactive process or transaction between a person and an environment (which is often another person)."[54] Robinson denies that rationality is the only tool for

---

[53] Ibid., pp. 206-207.

[54] Jenefer Robinson, *Deeper than Reason*, (Oxford University Press, 2005), p. 273.

understanding the world and the arts. Her work answers the super-rationalistic, philosophically realist position of Kivy, and also Stephen Davies's view that the structure of music reveals any meaning or truth about the work. Robinson states, correctly in my view, "for the past hundred years or so, music theory has been dominated by a formalistic aesthetic that has tended to denigrate the importance of emotion in music." [55]

Kivy cites a Bach choral prelude to support the claim that the meaning of some musical works is purely musical. He attributes the meaning of the piece to the composer's mastery of contrapuntal technique. However, Kivy also introduces an excerpt from Albert Schweitzer's *J. S. Bach*,

> He appears to have passed his last days wholly in a darkened room. When he felt death drawing night, he dictated to Altnikol [his son in law] a chorale fantasia on the melody 'Wenn wir in Hochsten Noten sind' [when we are in greatest need], but told him to head it with the beginning of the hymn 'Vor deinen Thron tret ich allhier' [I step right here before your throne], that is sung to the same melody...In the dark chamber, with the shades of death already falling round him, the master made this work, that is unique even among his creations. The contrapuntal art that it reveals is so perfect that no description can give any idea of it. Each segment of the melody is treated in a fugue, in which the inversion of the subject figures each time as the counter-subject. Moreover the flow of the parts is so easy that after the second line we are no longer conscious of the art, but wholly enthralled by the spirit that finds voice in these G major harmonies. The tumult of the world no longer penetrated through the curtained windows. The harmonies of the spheres were already echoing round the dying master. So there is no sorrow in the music; the tranquil quavers move along on the other side of human passion; over the whole thing gleams the word "Transfiguration."[56]

Here I would like to point out some different levels of access to the meaning of a musical work. One level is the knowledge and appreciation of the composer's skills. Bach's writing impresses us with its greatness just by hearing it. Another level is that of the historical facts. Kivy cites the above passage with information that goes beyond the music, namely, the circumstances in which

---

[55] Ibid., p. 293.

[56] Albert Schweitzer, *J. S. Bach*, quoted by Kivy, Music Alone, pp. 205-206.

the work was conceived and how its content is related to that situation. A third level is the performer knowing or not knowing these facts. Let us leave aside further levels, such as performing while knowing that the critics or audience know the historical facts, which then creates an expectation from the performer.

However, does it help a performer searching for a meaningful performance to know the circumstances in which a piece was written? This is an accepted idea among musicians. That is why we study music history and performance practices. Bach was dying when he wrote this piece. Can we access some meaning of "transfiguration", some quality of performance "on the other side of human passions" as Schweitzer describes it, just by focusing our attention on the music and its content, or its form? It is true that music expresses meaning through its musical form. Possibly if Bach's prelude form would have not been so close to perfection in terms of form, the meaning that Schweitzer found would have been different. Still, I would say that the form succeeds as long as it conveys meaning. In other words, I doubt that the musical form is the ultimate meaning. For example, Charles Rosen speaks of works by Franz Schubert as stylistically "degenerate" but having "virtues of their own that more efficiently organized music can rarely achieve."[57] Few musicians, if any, would deny that Schubert is among the greatest composers even though he might not match Kivy's objective standards of craftsmanship as the "exploration of musical possibilities within some given set of stylistic parameters."[58]

I will present another example to further the questions raised in the last paragraphs. This passage is from Maynard Solomon's *Beethoven*,

---

[57] Charles Rosen, *The Classical Style,* (New York: W.W. Norton and Company, Inc., 1971), p. 455.

[58] Kivy, *Music Alone*, p. 212.

> That the meaning of music is not translatable into language is a philosopher's truism. Kierkegaard wrote that music "always expressed the immediate it its immediacy" and that it was therefore "impossible to express the musical in language". And Nietzsche, in *The Birth of Tragedy*, noted that "language, the organ and symbol of appearance, can never succeed in bringing the innermost core of music to the surface. Whenever it engages in the imitation of music, language remains in purely superficial contact with it." Such warnings, however, have never stopped commentators (including, I fear, this one) from putting forth improvable speculations as to the 'meaning ' of one or another of Beethoven's masterpieces. Nowhere has this tendency been more manifest that in the nineteenth-century interpretations of Beethoven's Seventh Symphony. Berlioz heard a "Ronde des Paysans" in the first movement; Wagner called the symphony the "Apotheosis of the Dance"; Linz saw it as a second Pastoral Symphony [Beethoven's programmatic Sixth Symphony], complete with village weddings and peasant dances; Nohl visualized a Knight's Festival and Oulibicheff the masquerade or diversion of a multitude drunk with joy and wine. For A. B. Marz it was the wedding or festival celebration of a warrior people. More recently, Bekker called it a 'Bacchic orgy,' and Ernest Newmann described it as the "upsurge of a powerful Dionysian impulse, a driven intoxication of the spirit."[59]

Here we have several eminent critics expressing their opinions. Each one of them tried to put into words the meaning of Beethoven's work. It is interesting to note that Solomon compares them and realizes that in spite of the different free-associations, their imagery represents variations upon a single theme: a carnival or festival which "from time immemorial, has temporarily lifted the burden of perpetual subjugation to the prevailing social and natural order by periodically suspending all customary privileges, norms and imperatives."[60]

Solomon's last comment seems very close to Kristeva's idea that music seems to challenge the symbolic world. It is also reminiscent of Didier-Weill's concept of music cutting the circuits of words and their representations to address the representation of a drive. Solomon's comment also suggests that music could have a common meaning for many people.

I think we can answer now the question raised above-- whether is it the work or the emotions the work arouses in us that conveys the powerful meaning of music-- by saying that our emotions by themselves are the result of our interaction with the music. They are the byproduct

---

[59] Maynard Solomon, *Beethoven,* (New York: Schirmer Books, 1977), p. 212.

[60] Ibid., p. 212.

of the *musical experience.* Music, some instrumental music, I argue, seems to create similar emotions and furthermore a similar meaning for different people. I don't think this is threat to our subjective freedom. Many performers experience this in chamber music. We can all have different ways to express our subjective feelings and meanings of the music but at the same we relate to an object that has its own characteristics. Nevertheless, it is true that our culture and education might condition us to similar views. There is a tension here, a paradox, between the concepts that instrumental music, as a structured object, has an existence that imposes on us a certain meaning and the preconceptions of our culture. To the question raised above: Is there something else, an "existential", universal, quality of music? I might add, why is it that some music makes us feel as if we have a better understanding of reality?

For Didier-Weill, the universal quality, our "brotherhood", is the revelation of a drive and of a lack, which is a revelation in the order of our psychic constitution. The something else, for Kristeva and Didier-Weill, is a sense of understanding of a Real that was veiled to us before. This drives moves us to the Real that Didier-Weill calls the Blue Note. This tells us something about ourselves, within the framework of our subjectivity. The Real that music reveals is a meaning that is beyond language. In Dahlhaus's words, "[Music] contained a surplus in which one sensed its nature."[61] Instrumental music has a "surplus" of extra-musical meaning, this quality of allowing us to enter the realm of the sublime.

My point in this study is that this surplus or quality of existential revelation of music is related to the unconscious, to these realities of the sensible that cannot be perceived by our conscious being or our common sense. Music reveals to us the no-sense of life. I think the

---

[61] Carl Dahlhauss, cited above, p. 63.

formalist Kivy and also to some extent Robinson, miss this point. According to Kivy aesthetic value posses a problem for the purist,

> I must end here on a note of mystery and puzzlement. Those of us who cultivate a taste for the instrumental music of the West seem to find certain examples of it so compelling and of such enduring interest that "profound" forces itself upon us as the only (and fully) appropriate to describe them. Yet there seems to be no rational justification for our doing so. For even if the works we describe as profound [meaningful] have a subject, and that is debatable, the only subject matter they can plausibly be thought to have, namely musical sound itself, does not bear, at least on the face of it, any obvious mark as freedom of the will or the problem of evil, love and marriage, or crime and punishment, and so forth: the subjects of "profound" literary works[62].

To end this exploration of formal criticism I would like to stress three points. The first is that to have a better understanding of the musical experience is necessary to go beyond pure rationality. Since Freud we have known that culture exerts its influence over the individual, creating rules and norms that repress the satisfaction of drives. However, music and other artistic and scientific disciplines escape the repressive influence of culture and they produce breaks allowing the existence of new realities. Psychoanalysis, in addition to being a therapeutic treatment with roots in its theory about our psychic structure and processes, is a technique of investigation to access the deepest level of our mind and our culture. Through its light we can access further knowledge of music as one of the most fundamental human activities.

Second, with Lacan and his three dimensions of the Symbolic, the Imaginary and the Real, we have a deeper insight so as to know that many of our drives come from our mind and are expressed in our cultural body. The drives do not need an object in reality to create emotions or affective states. In this light, Kivy's claim that music does not have an object is proved false. Even depression or anxiety are often states of mind that do not necessarily have a "real", tangible object or reason. Instead, the cause is often repressed in the unconscious. Music as an object, the creation of a cello and piano sonata for example, comes from the Imaginary. The meaning of

---

[62] Kivy, *Music Alone*, p. 217.

music relates to a Real. Musical meaning is not about the emotions it arouses. Instrumental works, as we have seen in this study, have an existence; they constitute an object to which we relate in the performance situation.

The third point that I would like to address is the need for a new aesthetics to discuss the musical experience, to elaborate about the sensible. I think that many instrumental musical works for us performers or listeners do create a referent for our emotional response as real as any Dostoyevsky story. I agree with Robinson about the necessity of walking a path that defies rationality as the only tool for understanding the performing experience. Robinson's approach is based in the framework of cognitive psychology. This paradigmatic world of reference leads Robinson to present her theory of the "persona" in music to explain musical emotions. A persona for Robinson is the "other" that music represents for us, which would explain or make clearer to listeners the meaning of music. Alternatively, following Didier-Weill, I presented the invocative drive which is inscribed in the dialectic of the subject and the Other. This dimension of the Other functions at several levels: in the musical work itself but also in the sound of our voice or instrument, the audience, the chamber music partner, etc. All these instances create the otherness of the musical experience. I think that the psychoanalytic conception of the Other is a far richer explanation than Robinson's notion of "personae" to account for the other that a musical work represents. Cognitive psychology and other schools of "ego" psychology fall short in explaining many human manifestations. They mostly work on the surface of monitoring knowledge already established. In other words, if the musical and the performing experience are related with the experience of the sublime, the way for them to be accounted for is through a theory that includes the unconscious.

Phillip Merikle, psychologist at the University of Waterloo in Ontario, Canada, is one of the most prestigious researchers of the unconscious,

> Often we affirm that mind and conscious are synonyms, that we are aware of what is important for our survival. But the more we study the human unconscious the more we realize how much of what we are aware escapes our conscious state. Many acts of the daily life show us the presence of this "other me" that is the unconscious.[63]

This dimension of our existence is present while performing, composing or thinking about music. The meaning of music and the profound emotion we feel in experiencing some works, along with musical and body gestures are to some extent expressions of the unconscious. As with the mystic, in his experience of union with the universe, the musical experience blurs the limits between the performer and the music, or between subject and object. It is necessary then to try new approaches to describe the sensible features of the object. The need for a new aesthetics will be clear in an attempt to articulate the notion of the sublime.

The Sublime: Kant and Later Thinkers

I will now present a brief discussion of the concept of the sublime and its relevance in the performance of music. The term sublime is related to sublimation, and comes from the Latin *sublimis*, which means "uplifted." Edmund Burke, who was responsible for the development of the sublime as an important aesthetic principle in art, described the concept of the sublime in 1757 in his book *Philosophical Enquiry into the Origin of Our Ideas of the Sublime and the Beautiful* as something grand and dangerous - so grand and dangerous, in fact, that it cannot but

---

[63] David Maldavsky, (2001). *Investigación en procesos psicoanalíticos*, (Buenos Aires, Ed. Nueva Visión, 2001), p. 22.

evoke feelings of dread or veneration.

Before Hegel, the aesthetic was most fully described by Kant's *Critique of Judgment:* it involves the effects that representation of the object produces in the faculty of soul and what happens there only. The aesthetic experience culminates in registering the condition that establishes the universal communication of the judgment of taste. Kant thought that in this way, an object affects our perception independently of whether the object exists or not. Kant's critical philosophy marks out two distinct domains: the transcendental realm of *a priori* forms and the empirical realm of sensible matter. One of the major points of his philosophy is the articulation of the process by which the *a priori* structures of human subjectivity are mapped onto the sensible, phenomenal domain.

In the *Critique of Pure Reason,* Kant claimed that the sensible can only be received in a form by the structure of the human understanding. However, in *The Critique of Judgment,* he is surprised by the capacity of the sensible to manifest structural organization beyond that which the understanding can conceptualize in terms of the object's form. I think music is a manifestation of this sensible since it can be understood without a definite conceptualization. We can analyze a string quartet, for instance, with the tools we have and have some appreciation of its structure. Its meaning though, articulated in words, ultimately escapes us.

The understanding, for Kant, finds structure only in subsuming the particular under a general concept, never in the particular itself. This is the methodology of both science and music theory, which search for patterns and laws to relate to the object. We can study and measure the melodic design, harmony and the form in Beethoven's 5th Symphony, for example, but we cannot measure the profound impact we experience while performing or listening to it. Yet, according to Kant, the sensible (like Beethoven or Schubert's music) can manifest a regularity even though it does not have recognizable specificities. This regularity cannot be traced back to any concepts the understanding already has. The aesthetic experience of the beautiful is one example of such regularity in the particular. We find a single rose beautiful, not roses in general, because of a certain harmony or proportionality that appears to us in it.[64]

Before going on, I should mention that in Kant the beautiful is distinguished from a second kind of aesthetic experience, the sublime. The sublime involves a pleasurable experience in which the intellect is overcome by an object incomprehensible to our imagination. Kant speaks, for example, of appreciating a vast storm at sea or the great expanse of the pyramids. We are uplifted by realizing that we can take in such a vast object despite being unable to form a conception of it. In Kant's conception, it is the faculty of our imagination, during, for example, the performance of a Bach cello suite, that allows an encounter with the sublime, rather than conceptual thinking.

Some works of Beethoven's music can be considered sublime in the sense that they can transport performers and audiences into a kind of metaphysical ecstasy. Beethoven's 9th Symphony is remarkable in this respect. In its extreme length, insistent dissonances, juxtapositions, obsessive repetitions and overwhelming fortissimos, the music moves us in a profound way. Though we have become accustomed to many features of Beethoven's style, the music can still make us catch our breath.

Daniel W. Smith, in his article "Deleuze's theory of sensation: overcoming the Kantian

---

[64] Immanuel Kant, *Critique of Judgment*, trans. Werner S. Pluhar (Indianapolis and Cambridge: Hackett Publishing Company, 1987), p. 509.

duality"[65] tells us that there is a moment of phenomenology in Kant's sublime that opens aesthetic comprehension to a kind of dialogue between the empirical and the transcendental, instead of a communion in one direction only (as in cases of science or religion explaining the world). The idea is that one's choice of a unit of measurement reflects the object to be measured, just as this unit of measure influences the account of the object taken. The notion of a unit of measurement of the sensible brings a new notion of proportionality. Thus, the relation between the shared sensory world and the qualities of an object is not entirely prefigured by one end of the equation. This moment of change of mode of being, to name it in some way, is the phenomenological moment that allows Kant to experience an aesthetic encounter with the sublime.

The need for a new aesthetics is related to that proportionality: the account of the musical meaning through analysis vs. through the experience of music. In experiencing music, the flow of the music creates encounters with the sublime, understood as moments in which there is no synthesis. Common sense leaves space for a new awareness.

Schopenhauer revisited the concept of the sublime using his own terminology. He thought that the feeling of the sublime was identical with that of the beautiful, but they are differentiated by their relationship to the human will and in their level of intensity. He says that the difference between the sublime and the beautiful is that

> pure knowledge has gained the upper hand without struggle...and not even a recollection of the will remains with the sublime. Pure knowing is obtained first of all by a conscious and violent tearing away from the relation of the same object to the will which are recognized as unfavorable, by a free exaltation, accompanied by consciousness, beyond the will and the knowledge related to

---

[65]Daniel W. Smith, Deleuze, *theory of sensations: overcoming the Kantian duality*, in Deleuze: *A critical reader*. (Oxford and Cabridge: Blackwell Publishers, 1996), pp. 29-56.

it."[66]

Why do some performances convey the sublime? Possibly it is related to the work performed but also to the performer. Hearing Rostropovich in concert once put me into a particularly inspired mood for several days. I always wondered why some performers like Casals, Rostropovich, and Gould, among others, seem to perform almost as a religious revelation. What is behind such a meaningful performance? In Daniel Baremboim's words,

> Often we think that music is mainly about emotions between human beings (such as love, sadness, fury)....But in absolute music, one has to be aware that [music] is also an expression of the individual with himself, an expression of the individual and his relation with the world, with the universe.[67]

I think some performances are meaningful, sublime, because the composer and performer reveal a new dimension in their interpretation. For Schopenhauer, in the aesthetic state, normal categories and concepts of perception are suspended, thereby enabling us to become alive to usually unnoticed aspects, to "the significant form" of the object.

Nietzsche followed Schopenhauer's ideas of the sublime closely but had a different insight. In *Ecce Homo*, he states that in the sublime one experiences courage in the face of "horror and terror of existence"[68]. Nietzsche stresses that art is to be of service to life, whereas Schopenhauer stresses that art enhances, among other things, pure "objective" perception of the ideas (or, in the case of music, of will as such). Instead of a complete destruction of the subject, as seems to be

---

[66] Arthur Schopenhauer, *The world as Will and Representation*, Vol. 1 tr. E. F. J. Payne (New York: Dover, 1966), p. 20

[67] Daniel Baremboim, *Mi vida en la Musica,* (Buenos Aires: editorial Ateneo, 2003), p. 253.

[68] Friedrich Nietzsche, *Ecce Homo*, tr. R. J. Hollingdale (London: Penguin, 1992), p. 50.

the case in Nietzsche's Dionysian sublime, the Schopenhauerian aesthetic subject attains an exceptional state of purity that allows it to discover the (transcendental) conditions of life.

I extended this discussion of the sublime to Schopenhauer and Nietzsche because Schopenhauer's concept of will, like Nietzsche's concept of the will of power, the Dionysian and Apollonian, have had a great influence upon Freud, Lacan and French psychoanalysis. There is a link between these forces and the Freudian unconscious as well as the concept of will with the concept of the drive[69]. Barenboim's words coincide with many comments from famous performers and composers, and are reminiscent of Schopenhauer's idea of the sublime.

Let us return to Kant to summarize the need for a new aesthetics. For Kant the sublime shows a faculty of the mind surpassing every standard of sense. [70]To depart from him we could say that to conceive something that can be imagined or felt (like musical meaning) but not conceptualized is to come across a moment of friction between the faculties. This moment of friction would be a moment of experience beyond the common sense. Furthermore, its discovery by way of the sensible indicates that this moment is sensible nevertheless. Uncovered here is a kind of sensibility distinct from the daily life. If the sublime shows a faculty of the mind surpassing every standard of sense, perhaps musicians perceive and know more than what we think about the musical meaning.

---

[69] Schopenhauer's and Nietzsche's concept of the will contains the foundations of what in Freud became the concepts of the unconscious.

[70] Here I paraphrase and relate to music some arguments used in Daniel W. Smith, "Deleuze on Bacon: Three Conceptual Trajectories in the Logic of Sensation," in Gilles Deleuze, *Francis Bacon: The logic of Sensation*, tr. Daniel W. Smith (Minneapolis: University of Minnesota, 2002), pp. vii-xxvii.

A New Conception of Aesthetics

To continue the ideas expressed above I will present Deleuze's version of the moment of the sublime. For him, reflecting on Kant, the *cogitandum* appears when the faculty of understanding, pushing imagination always to find a measure, pushes imagination to its very limit and, at this limit, the imagination pushes back, leading the understanding itself to acquire a new power. Some musicians express in my opinion this coming back of the imagination to new horizons. In the realm of music performance, Rostropovich and his conception of sound or Gould's phrasing of Bach in his performance of *The Goldberg Variations*, unveil a similar insight into a new reality of the sensible. If they both recreate the sublime experience in their performances perhaps is because they offer an insight into a new dimension of expression, a new conception of sound and phrasing that is immediately felt but cannot be conceptualized *a priori* but only experienced. Their performances might be musically logical but not related to common sense or previous performance tradition.

For Kant's movement from the cogito to the *cogitandum*, Deleuze offers a similar movement from the sensible to the *sentiendum*, from the *perceptible* to the *percipiendum*. The *percipiendum* is that which forcibly erupts: it cannot but be perceived. Our unconscious symptoms would be a manifestation of the *percipiendum*, and so also would be Rostropovich's imagination of cello sound or Gould's feeling of voicing in the *Goldberg Variations*. I argue that just as Deleuze has illustrated in his concept of the *percipiendum*, the performing experience entails the connection to a different state of being.

To reflect on music I have proposed a revision in aesthetics. Aesthetics is no longer simply a "theory of nice feelings" (as Hegel put it) but a complex philosophy of art: it involves interpretation, criticism and reflection upon works of art. A work of art, such as a symphony, has an existence, a history, a place to be that constitute it as the object of the aesthetic or musical experience. In the first two chapters, we discussed music primarily from the point of view of the subject receiving the impact of the music. A philosopher who can be related to this tradition is Heidegger, who says, "We never wonder from the work of art but from ourselves. From ourselves, we never let the work be a work but we tend to represent it as an object that must provoke in us determined (mental) states."[71] I think Heidegger's thought is along the lines of what I suggested before: he shows the need to find a new way to interpret the sensible. I find a parallel idea in music when Cone writes that the judgments of our taste reveal the work of art as much as ourselves, "In the end, the critic himself must be willing to stand judged....all of us are revealed by our taste."[72] Some kind of subjective truth is involved.

Now, this new conception of the aesthetic involves more than a mere transformation in the history of ideas. It is not a mere inversion where the subject is changed by the objectivity of the work. Inversion for inversion's sake makes no sense according to Heidegger. The inversion requires that "we be prepared previously to see how this comes back to us in another way."[73] Philosophers like Deleuze have attempted to articulate the need for a new conception of the sensible. Another example is Jacques Ranciere. In his book *The Aesthetic Unconscious,* he presented the idea that the Freudian unconscious is based upon the notion of the aesthetic

---

[71] Heidegger quoted by Goldstein, *La experiencia estetica: escritos sobre psicoanalisis y arte*, (Buenos Aires, ed. Del Estante, 2005) p. 10.
[72] Eduard Cone, *The authority of Music criticism*, quoted by Patricia Herzog, p. 310.

[73] Heidegger, quoted by Gabriela Goldstein, p. 11.

unconscious.[74] He suggests the need for a new regime for the sensible. Aesthetics is not just a word, but it designates a terrain about works of art, such as musical works, and a specific way of thinking. This new regimen is a place where a specific way of thinking is built.

Ranciere's claim is that the Freudian theory of the unconscious is not possible unless is based on the regimen of thinking of the arts,

> this regimen of thought about [works of art] is that the one thing that characterize art, is an identity of a conscious action and one unconscious production, one desired action and an involuntary process.[75]

Ranciere's ideas support the need for a new understanding of music that goes beyond objective rationality. To me, his approach could be defined as an attempt to find a common ground between the acquired knowledge of music, performance tradition, and musical training and insights into the experience of music. In philosophical terms, we can see this "coming back to us" as revisiting and furthering (or even refuting?) Kant's views. In musical terms, the coming back consists of revisiting our performance tradition by confronting it with our experience of music, with our dreamed sound.

For Ranciere, the structure of the sensible, the empirical world around us, has a way of reverberating from its own conditions. Kant speaks of those conditions as *a priori* conditions, and he presented those conditions as universal structures of human experience. Ranciere's account of Kant mentions that his *a priori* structures are too historically embedded to be universal. Psychoanalysis, with its investigation of the realm of the unconscious, presents one variation of the measurement of the sensible.

Ranciere's argument finally conveys the need for a more complex account of the many levels that can be operative in our musical experience and musical understanding. Music involves the

---

[74] Jacques Ranciere, *L'inconscient esthetique*, (Paris: Ed. Galilee, 2001) P. 9.
[75] Ibid., p. 22.

simultaneous experience of conscious and unconscious discourses, what is said and not-said, what can be analyzed and what cannot.

In *The Politics of Aesthetics* Ranciere highlights the longstanding accounts of aesthetic production, such as Aristotle's, that have taken the properties of various areas of human culture-- determining which are the cause and formative force for the ordering of sensible to unfold. I can relate this to the tradition of harmonic analysis, for example. There is a causal power within matter itself to generate works of art. As Kivy would say, the logic of the musical structure is the object that tells us its meaning.

But Ranciere introduces a new level, a new insight different from Aristotle's or Kant's. Whereas for both of these philosophers, a faculty of the soul and *a priori* power of the subject, respectively, give to matter its sensible form; whereas for Ranciere, individuation, the subjective truth, is immanent within matter itself. As I said at the beginning, this is a truth in which the subject is existentially engaged, as if it could be our own sound or phrasing. For us musicians, these individuations, take the form of a gesture, a movement of the wrist, a sensation of weight. We all, performers and audiences alike, receive the impact of these individuations. As with Heidegger, Ranciere insists that it is not crucial to substitute one aesthetics for another aesthetics but to bring the two worlds together. I understand this as a continuous interchange of our tradition and preconceived knowledge with our feelings and what can be said and not said about the performing experience.

Preliminary Conclusions

In this chapter I have studied the musical object, formalist theories of musical meaning (by Hanslick and Kivy), and Robinson's theory of musical emotion. I have objected to them and argued the need for a new aesthetics of the sensible. My introduction included a statement of a search for "a little more truth" and proposed that psychoanalysis might help performers and musicians in general to explore musical meaning. I presented Robinson's ideas on the need for a path of defying rationality as the only tool for understanding the world and the arts. To have a better understanding of musical experience it is necessary to go beyond pure rationality. I feel that Kivy's emphasis on a cognitive description falls short of explaining the musical experience.

I presented a richer account for an exploration of the meaning of music under the light of psychoanalysis and from there a revision of the sublime, which begs in my view for the need of a new aesthetics.

Within the framework of the psychoanalytic theories of Kristeva and Didier-Weill there is a link between the musical experience and the sublime. Theodor Adorno said something similar, "In each genuine work of art something appears that did not exist."[76] As a matter of fact, the performing experience is one in which our conscious making of music occurs simultaneously with unconscious expression. The unconscious expression is revealed in details such as a gesture, a bodily movement or a sudden feeling of truthful communication.

---

[76] Theodor Adorno, *Teoria estetica*, (Madrid: Ed. Akal, 2004), p. 113.

Conclusion

In the first chapter I discussed Kristeva's theories considering the question of meaning and its structures in the speaking subject. Such an insertion of subjectivity into matters of language, music and meaning unfailingly led Kristeva to confront a semiology stemming from Saussure or Pierce with Hegelian logic and Lacanian principles. Her writing is aware of the splitting of subjectivity implied by the discovery of the unconscious, the breakthrough accomplished by Lacan in French psychoanalysis. The activities and performances of this subject are the result of a dialectical process. My study attempted to show that any rationalistic or positivistic approach to the question of musical meaning or the performing experience that tries to summarize stability where one should acknowledge mobility, or unity where there is contradiction, does not go deep enough. Kristeva proposes to analyze a signifying process, which presupposes a split subject. In other words, the object of her investigations is no longer language (as in structuralism), or discourse (as phenomenology would have it), or even enunciation; rather, it is the discourse of a split subject-- and this comes back to psychoanalysis.

Kristeva then, defines two types of signifying processes to be analyzed within any production of meaning: a "semiotic" one and a "symbolic" one. The semiotic process relates to the *chora*, a term Kristeva takes from Plato. The symbolic process refers to the establishment of sign and syntax, paternal function, grammatical and social constraints, symbolic law. The signifying process, as manifest in poetic language as well as music, results from a particular articulation between the symbolic and semiotic dispositions.

In brief, the performance of music is a practice that seems to open the space for representing the Real or the unnamable. My input was to add that just because we cannot articulate the meaning of music in words, it does not imply that music lacks meaning.

In the second chapter, in order to study music and the subject, I presented Didier-Weill's theory of the invocative drive. He begins with the fact that we are "touched" by music. It is as if, thanks to the music, we receive a certain response. He states that one way to understand the essence of the movement of the drive(s) is to be aware that the subject is moved by the revelation of the existence of a [structural] lack, a nothingness, a void sustained by what Lacan has called *the object a*. Music brings us a Real that was veiled to us before. Didier-Weill maintains that music provokes an emotion that has two movements, two states of mind simultaneously: a feeling of well-being and a state of nostalgia. We can neither measure nor understand the nature of this "nostalgic joy" *[jouissance]* that will arise in the instant that a note is played. This note is never monotonous even though it is always the same note. He named that note, that expectation, that promise of a pleasure that music evokes in us, the Blue Note. Didier-Weill concludes that music, rather than being a sublimation of a sexual drive, is more the expression of an experience of the sublime.

In this same chapter, I made a reference to the particularity in speech of my tone, my foreign accent, or the sound of my voice. This was another dimension of sound parallel to spoken meaning. The richness of the meaning of music is that it undermines the hierarchical structure of language. It allows us to perceive other levels or dimensions, namely, the dimension of no-sense, a newly discovered Real.

In Chapter Three I discussed the musical object, formalist theories of musical meaning (by Hanslick and Kivy) and Robinson's theory of musical emotions. I objected to them and argued the need for a new aesthetics. I mentioned that Kivy's emphasis on a cognitive description falls short of capturing the nature of musical experience. I would go even further: every time we are performing or listening and identify a musical moment with a word, such as "cadence", "Classical", or "brilliant", we undermine the musical experience. We replace the experience with a linguistic object that we refer as "music".

Music can reveal a Real. Under the psychoanalytic light it is possible to explore a new approach to the sensible, one that considers the unconscious and the imperceptible. Psychoanalysis presents us with a new way of looking at things---not only at music or art. It is in this way an aesthetic revolution, in the sense of a new regimen of what we hear (and see) in the world.

Musical works have represented an enormous value for each culture. In psychoanalytic terms we can say that music generates a *jouissance,* which for many musicians and non-musicians becomes on occasion an experience of the sublime.

The Performing Experience

Certain instrumental music creates a meaningful experience for us. We should neither underestimate the experience nor reject the idea of a hidden meaning or an experience of the sublime because we cannot explain it in scientific terms and because it escapes our common sense. The aesthetic experience is something that happens, something that is revealed to us when we are performing or listening. It is a point of encounter between a subject and an object, between rationality and the sensible, between reality and fantasy.

The aesthetic experience is, moreover, an experience of our senses, of the sensible. When some performance is meaningful to us it is because something of the order of the unconscious is revealed. This process happens with the interaction with the piece we are performing. And this object presents its own unique features to us. In fact, I agree with Barenboim, for whom a musical work once conceived by the composer leaves the Imaginary world of the composer to become "an energy" alive with its own essence.

In performing music, then, our mind and body sometimes overcome the states of mind of daily life. The conscious effort to control every note, to feel the weight or the pad on this or that finger, is somehow mixed with a selfless abandonment of the "I" of my everyday life. Perhaps, as Adorno said, I am "emptied" by the work and in a new zone of perception[77]. This intermediate zone has the quality of myself performing a clearly defined and well-know musical work (Rachmaninov cello sonata for example) that, however, will not ever be the same for another

---
[77] Ibid., p. 114.

performer. The fact that other performers and I go over the same notes, the same instrument, the same shared nature of an object (the musical work, the musical instrument) and, our performances yet remain always different, shows that a real property other than the thing's nature is in force in its being.

Ranciere's and Deleuze's aesthetics aim for a kind of communication and an example of a certain sensible force (ultimately the musical meaning) that goes unperceived from the too empirical perspective of either of two approaches: (1.) An Aristotelian conception that naturalizes historical contingent parts (as a scientific explanation of the musical meaning or the musical experience; or (2.) A Kantian aesthetics based on transcendental subjectivity founded in a logic that has a historical organization of the sensible (in the case of music, "Ego" Psychology schools or rigid schools of the performance tradition). To accept the paradox that the performing experience is ultimately unnamable, ineffable, is to articulate the dialectical process by which one perceives, remembers, and speaks about it. One paradox is that music appears to have an experiential, rather than a discursive logic. These words I have written have nothing to do with music *per se* (how could they?), but I think that writing, thinking and speaking of our experience is a valuable thing to do along with making music.

I am not trying to advocate the negation of language or of rational and traditional approaches to an understanding of music. Music theorists, historians, and aestheticians provide us with a significant contribution to understanding of the meaning of music. I am trying to articulate the need to convey and access the meaning and reality of what music history, theory, aesthetics and science *do not* convey or access. In other words, musical meaning can be understood immediately in the musical encounter without reasoning at all. Didier-Weill provides an insight about music and the subject but he tells us nothing about a particular work or type of music or music as an object. I think a source for understanding music as an object is the search for a new aesthetic of the sensible that might allow better articulation of the performing experience. I think this zone, this area of perception that the musical experience constitutes, becomes a drive for many performers in the sense of craving the sound, the emotion, the need of expression that we find in music. Whether or not that drive is inscribed in the circuit of drives, our cultural body or rather, it exists as a new mode of being which is beyond the circuit of drives I do not know and is beyond the purpose of this work.

I can only say that I share with my teacher and many colleagues and musicians of all time who wrote about it, the conception that performing music involves a quest for a certain truth to be achieved. And in order to make way for the meaning or the sublime experience or the truth to appear requires a certain state or mode of being (whatever you like to call it). In this increased state of consciousness (or unconsciousness?) language does more to negate the musical experience than to assist it. The performance of instrumental music, in the realm of the sublime, with its conscious and unconscious levels, can be then a way toward another state of being, a way to access the powers of music.

BIBLIOGRAPHY

Apollon, Willy. (1996) *Lacan: Politics and Aesthetics*. Albany State: University of New York Press.

Barthes, Roland. (1977) *Image, Music, Text* (tr. And ed. Stephen Heath) London: Fontana.

Beres, D. (1957) "Communication in psychoanalysis and in the creative process: A parallel". *J. Amer. Psychoanal. Assn.,* 5: 408-423.

Berezin, M.A. (1958) "Some observations on art (music) and its relationship to ego mastery." *Bull. Phila. Assn. Psychoanal.,* 8: 49-65.

Bychowski, G. (1951) "Metapsychology of artistic creation." *Psychoanal. Quart.,* 20:592-602.

Carbajal, Eduardo, Rinty D'Angelo, Alberto Marchilli. (2000) *Una Introduccion a Lacan*. Buenos Aires: Lugar Editorial S.A.

Chijs, A. Van Der (1923) "An attempt to apply objective psychoanalysis to musical composition." *Internat. J. Psycho-Anal.,* 4: 379-380.

Coker, W. (1972) *Music and Meaning*. New York: Free Press.

Coriat, I.H. (1945) *"Some aspects of a psychoanalytic interpretation of music.* "Psychoanal. Rev., 32: 408-418.

Dahlhaus, C. (1978) *The Idea of Absolute Music.* Chicago: University of Chicago Press, 1989.

Davies, Stephen. (2001) *Musical Works and Performances*. Oxford: Clarendon Press.

D'or, Joel, (1985). *Introduction a la lectura de Lacan*. Paris: Editions Denoel.

Edelson, M. (1975) *Language and Interpretation in Psychoanalysis.* New Haven, CT: Yale University Press.

Eggar, K. (1920) "The subconscious mind and the musical faculty". *Proceedings of the (Royal) Musical Association,* 47: 23-38.

Freud, E., ed. (1960) *Letters of Sigmund Freud.* New York: Basic Books.

Freud, Sigmund. (1887-1902) *The Origins of Psychoanalysis. Letters to Wilhelm Fliess, Drafts and Notes,* ed. M. Bonaparte, A. Freud, & E. Kris. New York: Basic Books, 1954.

_____ . (1927) *The Future of an Illusion. Standard Edition,* 21: 5-56. London: Hogarth Press, 1961.

_____ . (1930) *Civilization and Its Discontents. Standard Edition,* 21: 64-145. London: Hogarth Press, 1961

Germain, Paul. (1928), "La Musique et la psychanalyse." *Rev. Franc. Psychanal.,* 2:751-792.

Goldstein, Gabriela. (2005) *La experience estetica.* Buenos Aires: Del Estante Editorial.

Goodman, Nelson. (1976) *Languages of Art.* Indiana, Hackett Publishing Company, Inc.

Guberman, Ross Mitchell. (1988) *Julia Kristeva Interviews.* Columbia University Press.

Herzog, Patricia. (1995) "Music Criticism and Musical Meaning." *The Journal of Aesthetics and Art Criticism. Vol.* 53: 300-312

Ives, Kelly. (1998), *Art, Love, Melancholy, Philosophy, Semiotics and Psychoanalysis.* Kidderminster, England: Crescent Moon Publishing.

Kierkegaard, S.A. (1843) *De unmiddelbare erotiske Stadier; eller, Det Musikalish Erotiske.* Enten-eller, Copenhagen: C.A. Reitzel.

Kivy, Peter. (1990) *Music Alone.* Cornell University Press.

_____ . (1991) *Sound and Semblance.* Cornell University Press.

Koopman, Constantijn and Davies, Stephen. (2001) Musical Meaning in a Broader Perspective. *The Journal of Aesthetics and Art Criticism*. 59:3

Kristeva, Julia. (1974) *The Revolution of Poetic Language*. Paris: Seuil (tr. Margaret Waller).

_____ . (1980) *Desire in Language: a semiotic approach to literature and arts*, New York: Columbian University Press.

_____ . (1987) *Black Sun*. Paris: Gallimard.

_____ . (1989) *Language the Unknown: An initiation into Linguistics* (tr. Anne M. Menke). New York: Columbia University Press.

_____ . (1993) *Sensible Times*. New York: Columbia University Press.

Lacan, Jacques. (1966) *Ecrits I and II*. Paris: Editions du Seuil.

_____ . (1979) *The Four Fundamental Concepts of Psycho-Analysis* (tr. Alan Sheridan), ed. Jacques-Alain Miller. Harmondswoth: Penguin.

_____ . (1983) *Seminario II: El yo en la teoria de Freud y en la tecnica psicoanalitica*. Buenos Aires: Ediciones Paidos.

_____. (1986) *Seminario VII: La etica del psicoanalisis*. Buenos Aires: Ediciones Paidos.

Miller, Martin. (1967) "Music and tension." *Psychoanal. Rev.,* 54 pp. 141-156.

Minsky, Marvin. (1981) *"*Music, Mind, and Meaning.*" Computer Music Journal*, Vol. 5.

Muesterberger, W. (1962) "The Creative process: Its relation to object loss and fetishism." *Psychoanal. Study Society,* 2:161-185. New York: International Universities Press.

Muller, John and William Richardson. (1982) *Lacan and Language: A Reader Guide to Ecrits.* New York: International Universities Press, Inc.

Payne, Michael. (1993) *Reading Theory: an Introduction to Lacan, Derrida and Kristeva.* Cambridge, Massachusetts: Blackwell Publishers.

Rabate, Jean-Michel editor. (2003) *The Cambridge Companion to Lacan*. New York: Cambridge University Press.

Racker, H. (1951) "Contribution to psychoanalysis of music." *Amer. Imago,* 8: 129-163.

Ranciere, Jacques. (2001) *L'inconscient Esthetique*. Paris: Editions Galilee.

_____ . (2000) *Le Partage du sensible*. Paris: Editions La Fabrique.

Robinson, Jenefer. (2005) *Deeper than Reason*. Oxford University Press.

Schwarz, D. (1997) *Listening subjects: music, psychoanalysis, culture.* Durham: Duke University Press.

Salomonsson, B. (1989) "Music and affects: Psychoanalytical viewpoints." *Scand. Psychoanal. Rev.,* 12:126-144.

Shepherd, John and Peter Wicke. (1997) *Music and Cultural Theory*. Malden, Massachusetts: Blackwell Publishers.

Smith, Anne-Marie. (1998) *Language the Unknown: An initiation into Linguistics* (tr. Anne M. Menke). New York: Columbia University Press.

Vandenabeele, Bart. (2003) "Schopenhauer, Nietzsche, and the Aesthetically Sublime." *Journal of Aesthetic Education*, Vol. 37: 1.

Weill, Didier. (1984) *L'Ethique de la Psychanalyse et la question du cout Freudien.* Paris: Editions du Seuil.

_____ . (1995) *Les Trois Temps de la Loi.* Paris: Editions du Seuil.

_____ . (1998) *Invocations.* Paris: Editions du Calmann-Levy.

_____ . (2003) *Lila et la Lumiere de Vermeer.* Paris: Editions Denoel.

Zizek, Slavoj. (2003) *Jacques Lacan, Critical Evaluations in Cultural Theory.* Vol. I and II. New York: Routledge.

www.ingramcontent.com/pod-product-compliance
Lightning Source LLC
Chambersburg PA
CBHW071411290426
44108CB00014B/1770